FOR REFERENCE

HOW THE WORLD WEDS

To Claudia & Syp

Edgardo Simone

NEW·YORK 1·11·1928

HOW
THE WORLD WEDS

THE STORY OF MARRIAGE
ADULTERY & DIVORCE

by

Claudia de Lys

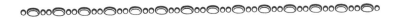

NEW YORK CITY

THE MARTIN PRESS

1929

Republished by Omnigraphics • Penobscot Building • Detroit • 1998

Library of Congress Cataloging-in-Publication Data

Lys, Claudia de.
  How the world weds : the story of marriage, adultery & divorce / by
Claudia de Lys.
    p. cm.
Originally published: New York : Martin Co., 1929.
ISBN 0-7808-0268-3 (library binding : alk. paper)
1. Marriage customs and rites. I. Title.
GT2665.L85 1997   97-15329
392.5--dc21   CIP

This book is printed on acid-free paper meeting the ANSI Z39.48
Standard. The infinity symbol that appears above indicates that the paper in
this book meets that standard.

Printed in the United States of America

CONTENTS

Part I

THE STORY THAT IS NEVER OLD

CHAPTER   PAGE

I. WOOING THE MAID . . . . . .   I I

Flowers in Courtship and Marriage—*Appeals* to the Other Sex — *Infant* Betrothals and Child-Wives—*Gifts* in Courtship and Marriage — *Dowry* and Trousseau Customs in Many Countries—*Serving* Time for a Wife—*Wedding* Proverbs.

II. TYING THE KNOT ROUND THE WORLD   43

Many Symbolic Ways of Tying the Marriage Knot—*Rings* in General—*Marriage* Customs of Shaving and Cutting the Hair —"*Banns*"—*Bridegroom*—*Bridesmaids*—*The* Wedding Dress—*The* Bridal Veil—*Orange* Blossoms as Bridal Wreaths—*Carrying* the Bride over the Threshold—*Rice* Throwing—*Shoes* at Weddings—*Wedding* Cake Customs—*Honeymoon*—*Lucky* and *Unlucky* Months and Days for Marriages — *Wedding* Superstitions in Many Lands—*Wedding* Anniversaries.

CONTENTS

Part II

STRANGE PEOPLES—STRANGE WAYS

CHAPTER   PAGE

I. REPENT AT LEISURE 109

Mother-in-Law Taboo — *Ancient* and
Present Punishments for Adultery—*A*
Few Customs of Divorce—*Widows* and
Widowhood in Many Lands.

II. YESTERDAY—EGYPT TO ROME . . 137

Ancient and Modern Marriage Customs of
Egypt—*Hebrew* and Jewish Marriage Cus-
toms — *Ancient* Marriage Customs of
Greece and Rome.

III. IN THE NORTHERN CLIMES TODAY 153

Marriage Customs of Scotland—*Germany*
—*Holland—Scandinavia.*

IV. SOME LATIN PEOPLES 167

Marriage Customs of Italy—*Spain, Portugal* and *Mexico—A* Few Marriage Customs
of France.

V. THROUGH EASTERN EUROPE . . 176

Marriage Customs of Switzerland—*Tyrol*
—*Hungary*— *Austria*— *Bohemia* — *Rou-
mania* — *Bulgaria* — *Russia* — *Russian*
Turkestan.

VI. NEAR EASTERN WAYS 197

Old Marriage Customs of Turkey—*Marriage* Customs of Armenia—*Syria—Persia*
—*Afghanistan.*

CONTENTS

Part III

SUPERSTITIONS AND FETISHES

CHAPTER   PAGE

I. IN THE DARK CONTINENT . . . 213

Marriage Customs of Abyssinia—*A* Few of the Many Marriage Customs of the Arabs —*Marriage* Customs of Morocco—*Kabyles* of North Africa—*Zulu-Kaffirs*—*Madagascar.*

II. FROM INDIA'S CORAL STRANDS TO CHERRY BLOSSOMS IN JAPAN . 228

The Different Forms of Marriage in *India* —*Marriage* Customs of *China*—*Korea* (*Chosen*)—*Japan.*

III. LITTLE KNOWN PEOPLES OF THE SOUTH SEAS 245

Marriage Customs of the Australian Aborigines—*Maoris* of New Zealand— *Samoa*—*Tahiti*—*Papuans* of New Guinea —*Malays.*

IV. MYSTERY PEOPLES 271

Marriage Customs of the *Gypsies*—*Marriage* Customs of the North American *Indians.*

PART ONE

THE STORY THAT IS NEVER OLD

CHAPTER I

WOOING THE MAID

FLOWERS IN COURTSHIP AND MARRIAGE

FROM time immemorial, flowers have been used as symbols of passion and devotion. Their colors and perfumes have been fashioned into a language which has made its way into the hearts of lovers and has been used ever since as a mode of expression during courtship.

The Greek lover adorned the door of his maiden with flowers and renewed them daily as a symbol of his admiration. To wear a flower signified betrothal; this custom was not only observed by the Greeks but by many other peoples. The bridal wreath worn at weddings evolved from the Greek and Roman rite of the corona nuptialis, nuptial crown, and formed a very important part of the marriage ceremonies. The present day ritual of the Eastern Church takes place with solemn grandeur, the priest placing a wreath on the bride and bridegroom's heads to signify honor and love. These wreaths originally were made of white and purple flowers entwined with olive-sprays and ribbons, but later they were composed of various other blossoms. Sometimes metal crowns, delicately designed, were used. The home of a Roman bride was always lavishly decorated with roses and marigolds, while violets were always the favorite flowers of the Athenians.

In Bohemia, the evening before the wedding, young girls, friends of the bride, assist in the making of the bridal wreath; each one adding a twig of rosemary and a prayer for the coming of her own mate. No man, except the future husband, is ever allowed to witness this ceremony.

In the Swiss Alpine villages, a bouquet of Edelweiss symbolizes courage as well as love, and acceptance by the maiden signifies that she will take him for a husband. In other parts of Switzerland, it is still the custom for a young peasant to place a rose and a billet-doux in a flower-pot on the window-sill of the young maiden's home. If, when she discovers the flower-pot and has read the lover's note, she does not take the rose, the lover is rejected, but, if the girl accepts it, the young man immediately enters and asks her parents for her hand.

In France and Italy, the preference is given to white roses, while in Germnay, red and white roses are entwined with myrtle leaves and offered during the period of courtship.

The primitive peoples on the Islands of the Pacific Ocean also express their emotions by means of wild flowers and leaves. A man who wishes to marry designates his desire by wearing a white flower over his ear; if his love grows ardent, he wears a red hibiscus. If his feeling wanes, he resorts to green leaves. In Polynesia, a woman wears a red hibiscus, given to her by the ardent admirer, over her ear to show the potency of her love.

The origin of scattering flowers in the path of the bride is lost in antiquity, but the tossing of the bride's bouquet is a relic of two old customs: that of throwing the bride's garter and stocking. A French superstition of the fourteenth and fifteenth centuries was that whoever caught the garter or stocking thrown by the bride was supposed to be the next one to be married.

In the language of flowers, a single blossom pressed in a book or letter is a declaration of friendship or love. The following is a partial list of the language of flowers and their symbols:

FLOWERS	SYMBOLS	COLORS	LANGUAGE
Acacia	Friendship	Yellow	I am beginning to love you.
Anemone	Perseverance	Blue	I am faithfully attached to you.
"	"	Red	I have faith in love.
"	"	Yellow	Will my love for you be rewarded?

FLOWERS	SYMBOLS	COLORS	LANGUAGE
Aster	Confident love	Blue and white	Believe in me.
"	" "	Lower part purple	I love you more than you do me.
Balsamine	Fragility	Delicate and mixed colors	I am worried, or You disdain my affection.
Slipperwort	Marriage	All colors	A proposal will soon be made, shall I hope?
Camelia	Pride	White	You disdain my love.
"	"	Red	You are the most beautiful of all.
"	"	Pink	I am proud of your love.
Carnation	Love	White	Believe in my friendship.
"	Admiration	Pink	I love you ardently.
"	Promise	Red	I have faith in your love.
"	"	All colors	I am your slave.
Dahlia	Gracefulness	Yellow	My heart is overwhelmed with joy.
"	Elegance	Mixed colors	All my thoughts are yours.
Daisy	Innocence	White or pink	You are the only one I wish to look at.
Forget-me-not	Faithfulness	Blue	I love you truly.
Fuchsia	Humble love	White and Red	Your love is my cult.
"	" "	Red	I love you with all my heart.
"	" "	Red and Purple	My love is constant and unshaken.
Gardenia	Sincerity	White	My affection is most sincere.
Geranium	Thoughts of love	White	You do not believe in me.
"	"	Pink	I am happy to be near you.
"	"	Red	You are forever in my thoughts.
Heliotrope	Attachment	White	I only wish for your friendship.
"	"	Purple	I still believe in you.
Hyacinth	Joyousness	White	I am very happy to love you.
"	"	Blue	The hope you gave me made me happy.
"	"	Pink or Red	Your love inspires me.
Iris	Tenderhearted	Blue	I love you tenderly.
"	"	White and Blue	I love and trust you.
"	"	Yellow	I am happy to love you.
Jasmine	Desire	White	Why do you begin to love me?
"	"	Yellow	I want to be everything in the world to you.
Lavender	Tenderness	Lavender	I love you with great respect.
Lilac	Tenderness	White	Let us love each other.
Lily	Purity	White	My sentiments are pure.
Lily - of - the Valley	Coquetry	White	You are beauty itself.
Mimosa	Sensitiveness	Yellow	No one knows I love you.
Narcissus	Egotism	White	You have no heart.
Orchid	Fervor	White	Pure love.
"	"	Orchid	Ambitious love.

FLOWERS	SYMBOLS	COLORS	LANGUAGE
Pansy	Affection	All colors	My thoughts are all yours.
Sweet Peas	Falseness	Blue or Pink	I do not believe in you.
Rose	Love	White	Anxious to love.
"	"	Pink	I make a vow to love you.
"	"	Yellow	Courteous attentions.
"	"	Red	Ardent love.
Sage	Esteem	Blue	I appreciate your qualities.
Tulip	Passion	All colors	A love declaration.
Violet	Modesty		Let no one know of our love.

APPEALS TO THE OTHER SEX

The discovery of ancient hollowed stone in Western Europe, supposed to have been used for the grinding of ochre, leads one to believe that prehistoric man and cave-dwellers had painted their bodies to attract a mate. Primitive peoples believed that red ochre had magical properties and would arouse love. Tattooing, used originally to designate race and tribal distinctions was so used, augmented by artistry, that it was considered alluring. It evolved into an essential requirement at the age of puberty among many primitive peoples; and was one of the most important formalities in their courtship and marriage customs.

A very interesting form of tattooing was practiced by the Egyptians. Their word Tattu means "The Eternal." They marked their bodies in order to carry through life and beyond death the sign which identified them in this world. It was customary for an Egyptian chief to have tattooed on his breast the animal representing the tribe to which he belonged; while the Egyptian women had their hands and feet tattooed for personal adornment and to denote their rank and quality. Tattooing and body-marking in Egypt were also practiced to symbolize fertility. Tattooing and painted designs giving evidence of pregnancy have been found upon female figures dating as far back as 2000 B.C.

Although the word tattoo is known to be of Polynesian origin, the custom was observed centuries before Polynesia was settled. It was undoubtedly practiced among the Hebrews, if we so interpret that portion of the Mosaic Law which prohibits the printing of any marks upon their bodies (Lev. xix. 28). The ancient Assyrians, Britons, and Thracians also practiced tattooing. It is still observed to-day in Arabia, as well as by the Chinese, Japanese, Burmese and North and South American Indians.

The Egyptian women used many cosmetics to make themselves more beautiful and seductive. They painted their faces with rouge and their fingers and toes with the juice of the henna plant. The same henna plant, used to transform raven locks into reddish ones, is much in vogue at present. Scents were used profusely by Egyptian, Greek, and Roman women as well as by the men; the hair was oiled and arranged in special coiffures to denote rank and quality. Kohl was lavishly used on the eyelids and eyebrows to make the eyes seem larger and more luminous. The allure of penciled eyebrows, vivid lips and rouged cheeks is not a new one; the use of the artistry of the boudoir is merely the continuation of world old customs contrived to lure and charm the opposite sex.

The many reasons for tattooing in Japan are quoted from Chamberlain's "Things Japanese" (p. 399): "A Chinese trader wrote that all men tattoo their faces and ornament their bodies with designs; differences of rank being indicated by the position and size of the patterns. But from the dawn of history, far down into the Middle Ages, tattooing seems to have been confined to criminals. This explains the contempt which the Japanese upper classes still hold toward tattooing. From condemned desperadoes to bravadoes at large, is but a step. The swashbucklers of feudal times gladly took to tattooing. A scene of bloody adventure, incised on the chest and limbs, impressed others with the bravery of the wearer. Other classes, whose avocations led them to bare their bodies in public, ornamented the entire torso with showy hunting, or theatrical scenes. In 1869 or thereabouts, the government made tattooing a penal offense."

Further, Mallery (418) gives the following seventeen reasons for tattooing:

1. To distinguish between free men and slave, without reference to the tribe of the latter;

2. To distinguish between a high and a low status in the tribe;

3. As a certificate of bravery exhibited by supporting the ordeal of pain;

4. As marks of a personal particular prowess;

5. As a record of achievements in war;

6. To show religious symbols;

7. As a therapeutic remedy for disease;

8. As a prophylactic against disease;

9. As a brand of disgrace;

10. As a token of a woman's marriage;

11. As a token of a marriageable condition;

12. Identification of the person, not as a tribesman, but as an individual;

13. To charm the other sex magically;

14. To inspire fear in the enemy;

15. To magically render the skin impenetrable to weakness;

16. To bring good fortune;

17. As the device of a secret society.

The Japanese tattoos illustrated their legends, mythologies, and national stories of their heroes. Their tattoo designs were very delicate and intricate and were so beautifully done that they created an illusion of a vividly colored costume clinging to the skin.

In Indo-China, the natives are so fond of ornaments and body decorations that they will suffer years of torture and will give to their bodies unnatural forms, such as the elongation of the ear lobes and the breasts. Girls, while still very young, begin to elongate their ears. They pierce them with a bamboo rod, sharpened for the purpose, and heavy weights are introduced into the holes; these weights are gradually increased as the ear lobes get longer. A suitor is proud to win the girl whose ear lobes are the longest. The lobes often hang to the shoulders, and sometimes the weights split the skin. This is equal to dishonor, and no girl with split ear lobes can ever get married. But the men of Indo-China practice the elongation of the ear lobes as well; and their love for brass and copper ear ornaments is extraordinary.

The desire to attract is a sexual one, and we know that the painting of the body, tattooing by puncture, scarification, and many other painful decorations, were all contrived for the purpose of charming those who might gaze upon them. They were not only religious and tribal symbols but they were also modes of expressing ideas of beauty through courage and endurance. This created heroes and made otherwise undesirable men the most sought after of the tribe. Those who stood the test of mutilation, were worthy of the admiration of the women whom they wished to marry.

In the following countries many weird modes of dressing and of ornamentation were practised. The scarring of the body and creation of deformities are still endured to lure one sex toward the other.

In Polynesia, while a man is being tattooed, the relatives sing and beat drums, to submerge the moans of the sufferer. Cries which the young man tries to control, show lack of courage. When the tattooing is completed, young girls congratulate the youth who stood the test, and who is now completely initiated into manhood.

The Marquesan women used to be tattooed on the ears, neck and lips, while the men had rings tattooed around their eyes and wore earrings and necklaces made of whales' teeth. Some of the girls have their names and nicknames tattooed on their arms and on their bodies as low as the waistline.

Among many of the Australians, at the age of puberty, the boys' teeth of the upper jaw are knocked out because the girls consider the conspicuous white teeth ugly. Others file them, to exemplify their manhood. Each family or tribe has its particular emblem or kobong tattooed on the thigh so that it may be easily recognized. The present lodge pin serves the same purpose!

In Ponapé, one of the Caroline Islands of the North Pacific Ocean, tattooing is practiced exclusively for the sake of ornamenting the bodies and to create sex attraction.

The Papuan women of New Guinea prefer large breasts. They wind many girdles round themselves to appear larger than they are. This is done to excite the admiration of the men and to provoke their comment on the beauty of the designs. The women of that region will not choose fat men, who therefore suffer any amount of pain to reduce the size of their waists. The native women believe that a small waist will require less food; and since they have to provide the greater part of the sustenance, they choose thin-looking men.

Samoan and Fijian mothers flatten the babies' noses with their thumbs and press their foreheads to force them to grow into a specially admired shape. The Samoan men are tattooed, but the women are not. The American Indian mother, also, places a board on her baby's forehead to prevent it from growing round. A receding forehead is the characteristic charm of the Indian. Tattooing was prohibited in Tahiti because of the obscenities and the unrestrained licentiousness which took place at the initiation ceremonies of those who had reached the age of puberty.

The Dyak women of Borneo also endure having their bodies tattooed in complicated designs. The more elaborate these tattoos, the more admiration they command and the easier it is to find husbands.

The native Carib women's legs are usually enormous in size. This is due to a special treatment which is started when girls are very young. Pieces of cotton two inches wide serve this purpose. One strip is knotted around the ankle and another below the knee, so that the leg in between may grow and bulge to please the Carib men who see in the thickness of the woman's legs her greatest physical charm. Aside from that peculiar custom, all body hair including the eyebrows, is plucked out. This latter custom is practiced by both men and women. For more adornment, the woman has her lower lip pierced, and pins of wood are inserted through it to form a special design around the mouth, while some of the Carib men have bell-shaped ornaments held by strings hanging from their lower lips.

The native women of Paraguay tattoo their faces to indicate their rank. Ashes mixed with blood are pricked into the skin with a sharp thorn. They use appendages to elongate their breasts. During the tattooing ordeal, a woman who weeps or cries out because of pain, is looked upon as a disgrace to her family and as not worthy of a husband.

The Maoris of New Zealand are reputed to be one of the most skillful peoples in the art of tattooing. Their patterns and designs are not only elaborate but are also very artistic and may well compare with those of the Japanese. Each graceful curve of the body is emphasized by the voluptuous design. Their lips are tattooed in blue. This is one of the most painful self-inflicted mutilations for the sake of creating admiration.

In India, a Brahmin woman paints the exposed parts of her body with a deep yellow cosmetic of saffron to appear more desirable in the eyes of the Hindu men who evince a susceptibility for that sort of sallowness.

The men of Laos, central Indo-China, have their bodies tattooed merely to please the women who admire signs of courage. The women of Behar, Hindostan, have rings of brass fitted to their legs. These are heavy and are serrated all around the edges. They are fitted on the legs with the aid of a hammer, while the woman writhes in pain upon the ground. Women of the lower caste wear bracelets of bell metal, often up to the elbow. The greater number of bangles, the more attractive the wearer is considered.

The Afghan women in south central Asia,

wear their hair as their tribal fashion dictates and to show whether or not they are married. Some of them tattoo blue marks on their foreheads. Bands of silver coins which decorate their foreheads are a sign of beauty and of wealth. The hair is usually arranged in two tresses, and a silken tassel dangles from the end of each.

In Africa, each tribe has its own characteristic ornaments to attract attention. The Galla women wear ringed adornments often weighing from four to six pounds. Some women of the Congo Bank wear metal decorations whose weight forces them to lie down at intervals to rest. Others who wish to be known as smart African belles wear large rings of copper which get very hot in the sun. A special attendant follows the girls for the purpose of moistening these rings to cool them.

Iron being a rare metal there, the Herere women of southwest Africa, have bracelets and anklets made of it, some weighing as much as thirty-five pounds. They are compelled to walk very slowly in an erect position. This carriage is looked upon by the native men as being very seductive. Those of the poorer classes, eager to attract male attention, though they themselves wear only a pound or less of the precious metal, mimic the strutting of the wealthy whose arms and legs are loaded with iron ornaments.

The men of South Africa wear rings of ivory

on the upper arm, the number designating the amount of wealth. Sometimes the arm is entirely covered with them. Nose-rings, or any other ornaments pierced through the septum, are a favorite fashion among them. Bracelets and necklaces of leather are also worn by both men and women. Raised scars which are colored to please the women are distinctive decorations. This scarraising is also practiced by many of the Australians. In Eastern Africa, the women wear lip rings, because native men think that these enhance their beauty; and the larger the ring, the more the women are admired.

In comparison with the other natives, the Hovas of Madagascar are a very light colored people and in order to look fairer and to emphasize the contrast, they paint dark spots on their cheeks.

Some of the Christian women of Bosnia have a Latin cross tattooed on their forearms to distinguish them from the Mohammedans. This practice has existed since the twelfth century.

Throughout the ages the desire to attract a male has led both men and women to do atrocious things at the risk of being deformed for life.

Just recently, the corset was announced to have been the cause of seventy-five per cent of the bladder trouble in women, not omitting the dangers which loomed at childbirth. All this self-

torture was endured because of the inheritance
of the universal belief that decorations, ornaments and the subjection of the shape of the body
to style dictates, stimulate the desires of the opposite sex. The pain is forgotten in the success of
the lure.

INFANT BETROTHALS AND CHILD-WIVES

When the custom of infant betrothal is practiced, betrothal means marriage of both the boy
and girl at the age of puberty, without the consent of the youthful participants.

In India, boys of eight, seven and even six
years of age are betrothed to girls who are still
younger. The laws of Manu give a man the right
to marry when twenty-four years old, a girl the
right to marry when she is eight or nine; that
being about the age of puberty for girls in India.
An old Sanscrit verse proclaims that "the mother,
father, and eldest brother of a girl shall be
damned if they allow her to reach maturity without being married."

At one period the predominance of men in
India was enormous, and there were as many as five
million more men than women; girl infanticide
being the cause. The baby girls who were not disposed of with opium or as fresh prey to wild animals, lived to face a life which was often worse

than death itself. They were married to old men of sixty or more, often before they had reached the age of puberty. These child-wives worried because they could not bear a child for their husbands, and followed their masters about like diminutive slaves, with haggard faces and dwarfed bodies. If they could not bear a son, they were discarded.

In the code of Manu, a man of twenty-four may marry a girl of eight, or a man of thirty, marry a girl of twelve; but if she has not reached puberty, cohabitation is forbidden. Early marriages among the Hindus are contracted to protect themselves from promiscuity, and in order to have sons as soon as possible. They believe in a hell called "Poot", to which a man's soul will go unless he has a son who will deliver him from it; so that he may enter the Hindu Paradise. The English Government has done much to improve the inhuman customs of infant betrothals and marriages in India; but in spite of its continued vigilance, the Hindus manage to ignore the law. Dr. Rider says in her book *Little Wives of India*, "A man may be a vile and loathsome creature; he may be blind, a lunatic, an idiot, a leper, or diseased in any form; he may be sixty or seventy years old, and may be married to a child of five or ten, who positively loathes his presence; but if he claims her she must go. There is no form of slavery equal to it on the face of the earth." In the Indore State, central India, a new law has been enacted which prevents old men from marrying young girls. Those who disregard the law are imprisoned for a period of six months and are fined two hundred and fifty dollars.

Infant betrothals and marriages are practiced by nearly all the natives of the Pacific Islands. In the past, the Kanaka natives of New Caledonia betrothed a girl as soon as she was born; and even now the custom still prevails. In the Fiji Islands, girls were betrothed when three or four years old to men who were several times older. Those who were not betrothed when young, could choose their husbands and marry them without the consent of their parents.

The custom of infant-betrothal is practiced in the Malay Archipelago, New Guinea, Tahiti, Tasmania and Southern Australia. Borneans marry girls who are three or four years of age; the Javanese choose them at seven. In Sumatra, Celebes, Tonga, and Samoa, early betrothals are practiced.

In China and Japan, girls were formerly married when eight, ten or twelve years old. At the present time, however, the marriageable legal age is fourteen. In Ceylon, girls marry between ten and twelve. The North and South American Indians also practiced child-betrothals and early marriages. The Bushmen, Hottentots, Kaffirs, and Somals, betrothed the girls at the age of seven. Among many tribes of Madagascar, such as the Bechunas and the Basutas, this custom prevails at the present. Among the Hovas the girls marry at a much later age.

In Egypt, child-wives of seven and eight years are no longer seen; the marriageable age being about sixteen.

In Scotland, in 1600, infant marriages were so frequent that they were strictly forbidden by law; and the legal age was made between twelve and fourteen. In Spain and Russia, early marriages prevailed. France and England also sanctioned royal infant betrothals.

GIFTS IN COURTSHIP AND MARRIAGE

The desire to please has undoubtedly been an important reason for gift-making during courtship. In illustrious legends, as in many true stories, we often read of the priceless gifts given by the lover to the maiden whose heart he had won. It is claimed by some authorities, however, that this practice is a survival of marriage by purchase. Gifts as a price for the bride have become symbolized in the custom of presenting a coin at the marriage ceremony. This is observed in many countries.

To present gloves with three pieces of money in them was an old rite observed in the Middle Ages. These gloves were given to the priest officiating; he would place them in the bridegroom's right hand who, in turn, would place the gloves in the bride's right hand, thus making the first gift to his future wife, which gave rise to this saying:

"My wooing's ended, now my wedding's near
   When gloves are giving."

At one time, in ancient Germany, marriage was constituted as soon as the exchange of gifts had been made. In India, the parents of the bride and bridegroom provide the jewelry to be exchanged at the marriage ceremony.

The exchange of gifts is a very important formality at a betrothal and at the wedding in many countries. In Japan as well as in China, it is the binding symbol of marriage. After the gifts have been exchanged the union has become indissoluble. In China, a list of the gifts is included in the bridal contract.

In some parts of Bulgaria, the suitor gives gold and silver coins to the bride who wears them as a necklace. This is a form of announcing the betrothal.

In Timor, an island of the Malay Archipelago, a woman, wishing to be married, presents her lover with something which she has worn, such as a flower, a comb, or any ornament which has adorned her body. Among many semi-civilized tribes such as the Khakyens, Aru Islanders and Kaffirs, a woman who accepts a gift accepts the man as a husband. This constitutes the marriage ceremony.

In South Celebes, the bridegroom presents to the bride "a pair of ginger roots which have grown together", symbolizing the lover's wish of being as closely united in marriage with the woman of his choice, as the twin ginger roots. This gift is an important part of the marriage ceremony.

In Sweden, a girl gives the bridegroom a shirt made by her own hand; the bridegroom gives the bride as many gifts as he can afford. Knives, shoes, and handkerchiefs, are considered very unlucky for future happiness of the couple and are, therefore, never given.

When a North American Indian suitor wished to gain the favor of the bride's parents, he usually presented gifts of blankets, bracelets, and necklaces. If they were accepted, the parents agreed that he should marry their daughter. This constituted the betrothal. Among some of the Iroquois, the mother of a young girl led her daughter to her future mother-in-law and presented the latter with gifts of maize cakes. If the cakes were accepted the young girl became a member of the family immediately.

BRIDAL SHOWERS

The bridal shower is said to have originated in Holland, many centuries ago. A beautiful maiden wanted to marry a miller, who, because of his generosity to the poor of the village, had no fortune laid aside. Her father, who had selected a rich owner of pigs for his future son-in-law, naturally objected to the poor miller. Hearing the young man's sad story, those who had received his assistance, decided to help him in return. They each contributed what they could, so as to make the marriage possible. Thus, the "Dutch Shower" became a popular custom among all classes and in time evolved into a very important function. Later this custom spread to other lands, and it is much in vogue today.

DOWRY AND TROUSSEAU CUSTOMS IN MANY COUNTRIES

"Let her beauty be her wedding Dower"
Shakespeare

In Lydia, Western Asia Minor, and Phoenicia, it was customary for a maiden to sacrifice her virginity and to become a temporary prostitute, in order to earn her dowry. The virginity of maidens was offered to the goddesses of fertility, and the money derived from their offering was used for two purposes: either as a dowry or as a personal gift to the goddesses' temple. When their earnings enriched the treasury of the temple, Lydian girls believed that the protection of the goddesses who witnessed such generosity, would always be accorded to them. This money was afterward used by the temple priests, who enjoyed a leisurely life at the expense of the parents' and maidens' religious credulity. Later, when these practices assumed an entirely sensuous nature, they were abolished.

Lydian girls who earned their dowries in this manner, and those who gave all to the temple, were never looked upon as immoral. When they retired, they had no difficulty in finding husbands. Upon marrying, however, the temple girls who had donated all their earnings to the goddesses, expected every guest who had enjoyed their favors to give them a present. The custom of rewarding the bride for a favor exists in some parts of Europe to-day. For the bride's kiss or a dance, a gift is offered.

This custom of the sacrifice of virginity was a relic of the phallic worship which was practiced in the temple of Mylitta, where maidens offered themselves. It was not only prevalent in

Babylonia, but in many parts of Cyprus and in ancient Armenia. The temple dedicated to Juggernaut in India was also given over to these rites. Sacral harlotry is supposed to have been practiced in certain parts of Greece. It is said that this practice was also observed in Scandinavia previous to the tenth century; and many of the Incas of Peru instructed their daughters to earn their dowries in that manner.

In classical Attica, Greece, the dowry plays a very important part in the life of a girl. A father usually gave his daughter a tenth of his property. When a maiden possessed a dowry, she was acceptable as a wife; otherwise she assumed the state of a concubine. In Athens the dowry belonged to the wife, and the property of the husband could not be willed to the widow. Each had a right to their respective properties. The husband could pay for the marriage ceremony with his wife's dowry. In case of divorce or his death, it was returned to her.

A girl without a dowry was likely to remain unmarried. To avoid this condition, as soon as a girl was born, the parents started to provide for her future. In many cases, brothers saved their earnings and did not marry, until their sisters had been disposed of.

In ancient Greece, peasant girls wore headdresses decorated with strips of coins, a manner of displaying their dowries. This custom is still observed to-day in Algeria. When a woman is looking for a husband, she wears bands of European coins on her head for the sole purpose of inviting a proposal.

The custom of the *dos* or dowry in Rome became compulsory by the statute *Lex Julia* enacted just before the end of the Republic. The Romans, however, did not practice sacral harlotry.

In the event of divorce among Hebrews and Mohammedans, the dowry was returned to the parents of the bride.

Dowries have not always consisted of money. The trousseau and marriage chest which are brought by the bride as part of her dowry are popular even to-day among many peoples and races. There is still a superstitious belief that unhappiness is the fate of the bride who does not herself work on all of her trousseau articles. In Roumania and in Bosnia, girls start to prepare their trousseau when very young, as an inducement for the "wife-seekers." In Bulgaria and in Sicily, the trousseau is on display to all, one or two days before the marriage ceremony and always commands a great deal of comment. The ability of the girl, as well as the quantity of the objects and the quality of the materials with which they are made, are considered. Little girls start to work on their trousseau at school, and this work remains their main occupation until the day before they are married. All the linen is elaborately embroidered and finished with drawn-threads. The marriage chest in which the trousseau is placed is an object highly prized and preciously kept from generation to generation. This custom is also observed in Spain, although the trousseau plays a secondary part in the marriage contract, since Spanish girls may select their husbands themselves.

"If a bride cries before her marriage, she will not cry after it," is an old superstition, and in the hope of the adage's truth, in some countries the bride walks behind the dowry-cart, weeping all the way to the home of the bridegroom.

Among the Russian peasants, the bride lives with her parents-in-law and donates a piece of land as the dowry. In Siberia, the Koryaks always prefer as bride the woman who has the largest number of reindeer, for the animals are worth a great deal more than any other form of dowry.

In Morocco, a marriage contract includes a list of the articles which belong to the bride for her own exclusive use, and it gives her the right to claim these personal possessions at the time of her divorce or at the death of her husband.

Among the Syrians, a bride is given a certain

amount of money which goes toward her dowry.

In Europe, according to the "Code Napoléon," a dowry is unnecessary, but parents always provide a "dot" for their daughters and the custom is widely practiced, particularly in France. In some parts, when a girl is too poor to have a sufficient dowry to bring her the husband of her choice, her friends go about the village collecting gifts and rewarding the donor with a kiss. In Brittany, several days before the wedding, the trousseau and wedding gifts are exhibited for all to see. This is an occasion for dancing, singing and the playing of old games.

SERVING TIME FOR A WIFE

The old custom of "marriage for service," as mentioned in the Old Testament has not entirely disappeared, and still prevails among many tribes. Jacob procured for himself two wives by working for his uncle Laban fourteen years; seven years for each wife. The term of seven years is observed by the Hindu suitor who wishes to marry and cannot afford to pay for the wedding expenses. In that case, he donates his services and at the end of the seven years he is given one of the daughters in marriage. The father-in-law pays the wedding expenses and when the ceremony is over, the couple may go and live where they please. The bride and bridegroom, before going away, are given "a cow, a pair of oxen and two copper vessels (one for drinking, the other for their food) and enough rice to feed them for the first year of their married life."

In Ceylon, there is a similar custom called *beena marriage*, which compels the penniless suitor to give up his family ties and to live and work in the family of his future wife. Then his wife, children and parents-in-law live all together as one family. All his children are supposed to belong to his wife's family.

The Koryaks and Chukhis of northeastern Siberia are polygamous. In order to secure each wife, a Koryak works for his prospective parents-in-law for a certain length of time. After this period the daughter is given to him in marriage.

Many of the American Indians practiced this custom. The Mayan husband of Yucatan and Mexico built a house near that of his future bride's father and worked for him for a period of five or six years. Then he took the daughter as his bride. When a suitor of the Hupa tribe of California could not pay the customary amount of money in exchange for a bride, he worked for his bride's father for a stipulated period of time.

Among many tribes of Brazil, a suitor gives a year's service to earn a bride. At the expiration of that time, he may either live with his parents-in-law or leave them to build his own hut. Among other tribes, the bridegroom remains with his wife's family, but as soon as the couple is married, the bridegroom and father-in-law refrain from speaking to each other in accordance with an old and as yet unexplained taboo.

The most popular custom is for the lover to work a year to gain his bride. A suitor silently enters the home of the girl of his choice, bringing food and fire, and in answer to the query of her parents as to his desires, he makes known his wish to marry their daughter. Nothing more is said, and at the end of the year, he makes the girl his wife.

In Africa, the Bushmen, who are unable to pay for their brides, work a season or two for their parents-in-law, this service constituting the marriage ceremony.

The Annamites have a custom which they call "The Son-in-Law in the making", compelling the poor suitor to work for the family of his bride. As soon as the son-in-law has worked for the price of his wife—the ordinary price of a woman is rarely higher than the equivalent of fifty francs, they are both free to live elsewhere. This custom of serving time to earn a wife is still observed to-day among some of the peasants of the Haute-Savoie in France.

WEDDING PROVERBS

The following are a few of the typical proverbs pertaining to marriage in various countries.

English Proverbs

Refuse a wife with one fault and take one with two.

The calmest husbands make the stormiest wives.

He that hath a white horse and a fair wife never wants trouble.

Who marries for love without money has good nights and sorry days.

Italian Proverbs

In buying horses and in taking a wife, shut your eyes and commit yourself to God.

Before you run in double harness, look well to the other horse.

The first wife is matrimony; the second company; the third heresy.

Marriage comes unawares, like a soot-spot.

French Proverbs

He that hath a wife hath strife.

Marry your son when you will and your daughter when you can.

One marries a fool not to be fooled.

Scotch Proverbs

If marriage be made in heaven, some had few friends there.

A man may woo where he will, but must wed where he's wooed.

Chinese Proverbs

Ugly wives and stupid maids are priceless.

She who is wife of one man cannot eat the rice of two.

An ugly daughter-in-law cannot conceal that fact from her mother-in-law.

A maid marries to please her parents; a widow to please herself.

If heaven wants to rain, or your mother to marry again, nothing can prevent them.

Japanese Proverb

Honest people have many children.

Spanish Proverb

A man's best fortune, or his worst, is his wife.

Hebrew Proverbs

He who has no wife is no man.

"God did not make woman from man's head, that she should rule over him; nor from his feet, that she should be his slave; but from his side, that she should be near his heart." (*Talmud*)

Arab Proverbs

The love of a man for a woman waxes and wanes like the moon.

Marriage is joy for a month, and sorrow for life.

African Proverb

He who marries beauty marries trouble.

Hindu Proverb

A young wife should be in her house but a shadow and an echo.

Syrian Proverb

Girl, do not exult in the wedding dress; see how much trouble lurks behind it.

Maori Proverb

Let a man be ever so good-looking, he will not be much sought; but let a woman be ever so plain, men will eagerly seek after her.

CHAPTER II

TYING THE KNOT ROUND THE WORLD

MANY SYMBOLIC WAYS OF TYING THE MARRIAGE KNOT

HE "true-love" is a phrase derived from the Danish verb trulofa, i.e. fidem do, "I plight my faith or troth." The lover's knot is symbolical of love and duty and it represents an indissoluble union. It has been the emblem of marriage from the remotest times, and the tying of a knot is still practiced in various ways by different peoples as a symbol of love, affection, faith, friendship and duty. The tying of a knot at marriages, an old Danish custom, has been practiced by the English and the Scotch.

Among the Anglo-Saxons, the custom has existed in the ribbon-tied bouquet of the bride and bridesmaids, and the groomsmen's boutonières. In Pertshire, however, the bride and bridegroom had to loosen every knot on them before the wedding ceremony. The untying of the knots, it was believed, would loose the evil influence bound in them by any hand with sinister motives.

Among some tribes in Malakka, southeast

Asia, and also among many of the Indo-European people, the bridegroom leads the bride by the hand. Knotting each other by the hand in this manner is one of the most important ceremonies at their marriages. Among the Orang-Sakai, the little finger of the bridegroom's right hand is joined to the little finger of the bride's hand, thus making this human link the emblem of a chain symbolic of the bond for life.

At the marriage ceremony of the Romans, the bridegroom was obliged to unbind (so vere) the girdle of the bride, instead of tying it. This is the only instance in the history of marriage where the custom differs from the universal one of tying objects at weddings.

Among some tribes of Equatorial Africa, the survival of the "blood-letting rite" is evidenced when the suitor scratches the shoulders of the bride with his nails, until the blood appears. Only when the blood is visible does he feel that they are bound together in marriage. For the purpose, the man's nails are permitted to grow in preparation for that ceremony.

Marking the bride with blood is also observed in some parts of India. It is assumed by many to be the survival of the Hindu custom of marking the bride with red clay. A red powder called Sindur is still used. The binding ceremony of marriage takes place when the bridegroom has made a mark on the bride's forehead. It is usually a dot placed between the eyebrows. This mark is also indicative of a high caste. Among some of the Moï tribes of Indo-China, the marriage ceremony is concluded by a mutual scratching of the face.

In Mexico, the bride's veil is pinned on the bridegroom's shoulders symbolic of spiritual as well as material union.

In Sumer, a territorial district of Babylonia, threads from the garments of the bride and bridegroom are made into a knot to symbolize the marriage.

The Portuguese marriage ceremony is simple; the hands of the bride and bridegroom are tied together by the priest's stole before the ring is put on the bride's finger.

At the marriage ceremony of the Karans of Bengal, the right hand of the bride and bridegroom are bound together with a special string. Often the garments of the pair are tied together, while they go around the sacred fire three times. In Ceylon, the bride, who has twisted a thin cord, ties it round the wrist of the bridegroom; the belief is that as long as he clings to the string, he clings to his wife.

Among some of the Hindu tribes, the joining of hands and binding them with grass is the main marriage ceremony. This is performed by the priest. Among the Dyaks of Borneo, the ritual simply requires both the bride and bridegroom to sit on two iron bars holding hands. The tying of the tali in India is the binding formality which makes marriage indissoluble. The tali is a very small gold ornament strung on a short cord composed of one hundred and eight delicate threads twisted together. This cord is dyed yellow in saffron water. At the conclusion of the ceremony of the tali, it must be blessed by all the old women present whose husbands are still alive, to assure happiness and a long married life for both the bride and bridegroom.

The Parsee bride has her hands tied with the sacred cord seven times. Among the ancient Carthaginians, the bride and bridegroom had their thumbs tied with thin leather laces.

In ancient Hibernia, an old custom consisted of giving a bracelet woven of human hair to a maiden. Acceptance completed the marriage to the man who had offered this strange gift.

Among the North American Indians and among many tribes of central Africa, a strange practice existed. The man washed his hands and then the bride drank the same water to show her fidelity and love as well as to carry out the old primitive belief that the bride had tasted of the strength of the future groom.

Thus was the marriage knot tied around the human race.

RINGS IN GENERAL

The Ring of Mythology

When Jupiter forgave Prometheus for stealing sacred fire from heaven, he ordered him to make a ring out of one of the links of the chain with which he had been bound to Mount Caucasus and to place in its collet a piece of the rock at which he had been held. This is supposed to have been the first ring set with a stone.

Roman Rings

In Rome, the custom was to give to the bride on the point of a sword the ring which was then used as arrha or earnest-money. Sometimes, instead of using a ring as arrha, the bride and bridegroom drank and broke a gold piece together. The custom of breaking gold or silver as a pledge of the marriage pact was widely practiced by the lower classes; one half was kept by the man and the other half by the woman. This preceded the exchange of rings.

The iron ring used at the Roman betrothal

rites is said to have been originally the link in an iron chain. The Roman keys which can be seen in the British Museum to-day, are made with a ring-shaped handle linked together, worn on the fingers.

Juvenal informs us that, during a feast, the man gave the woman chosen for his future wife, a ring, annulus pronubus, which she placed on the fourth finger of the left hand as a pledge of marriage. This constituted the betrothal ceremony. The ring given at the betrothal was made of iron; the gold ring being a custom of a much later date. Among many Roman citizens, the bridegroom still practiced the giving of an iron ring long after the gold one had been introduced. Pliny says that during his time, a gold ring was given to the bride to wear in public; and later, another one of iron to wear indoors. Other historians say that heavy rings were worn in winter and lighter ones in summer. On the other hand, Tertulian hints that in ancient times, a ring of gold was used instead of an iron one.

However, in spite of this controversy, whatever metal was really used matters little; the fact remains that rings were given as a pledge at betrothals. The betrothal ring used as arrha became the engagement ring of to-day; and the wedding ring is merely a duplicate of the betrothal ring.

Egyptian Rings

In Egypt, gold was used in the form of rings before coinage was introduced, and these same rings were used at marriage ceremonies. The bridegroom would place a gold ring upon his bride's finger. This gave her the right to share with him his honor and estate. The gold ring used at weddings is a very old custom which was retained by the early Christians. At the Council of Trent, the survival of the pledge ring was not only recognized as being sacred, but it rendered the marriage legal, even without a priest's blessings.

The giving of the keys of the house as well as the bridal ring was formerly a custom among the Anglo-Saxons and the customary phrase was, "I give thee my daughter to be thy honor and thy wife, to keep thy keys," etc.

Fourth Finger for Ring-Finger

Macrobius, in his Saturnalia cites an explanation for the wearing of the ring on the fourth finger of the left hand, related to him by an Egyptian priest. The ring was placed on the fourth finger of the left hand at betrothals or at marriage ceremonies because it was believed that a nerve ran from the finger to the heart, thus giving the bridegroom the delightful illusion that he had placed a ring around the heart of the bride. This ancient tradition is undoubtedly the fabrication of an imaginative mind, for the fourth finger of the left hand has not yet been proven to possess a special nerve not found in the other fingers. But a fourth finger of the left hand is less active, and it is presumed that the ring was placed on that finger because there was less danger of injuring it. Another explanation is that the "wedding-ring is worn on the left hand to signify the subjection of the wife to her husband." The right hand signifies power, independence, and authority.

Greek Rings

Many nations have imitated the ancient Greek custom of wearing rings, while the Greek people themselves derived their custom from the Orient. Rings are not mentioned in the Iliad or the Odyssey; but there are many proofs which lead us to believe that they were used both by the Greeks and the Trojans.

The giving of rings at betrothal and at wedding ceremonies of the Greek Church, is very different from that practiced in other Christian Churches. Two gold rings are used; the bride and bridegroom each have one, worn on the fourth finger of the right hand, supposed to be on the side of honor. Formerly, the woman was given a silver ring and the man a gold one.

Hebrew Rings

Among the Hebrews, a ring was apparently used to seal orders and covenants, and also in time became the emblem of marriage. The ring given to a woman at marriage gave her the right to act in behalf of her husband, to dispose of property, and to represent her husband in every way. Josephus, in his third book of the Jewish Antiquities says: "The Israelites had the use of them (the rings) after passing the Red Sea, because Moses, on his return from Sinai, found that they had forged the golden calf from their wives' rings."

At first, Jewish wedding rings were made of plain gold, without jewels; sometimes silver or a less valuable metal was substituted. Often, wedding rings were so large that they could not be worn. A popular ring used during the sixteenth and seventeenth centuries had a delicately engraved design, representing the temple of Jerusalem. Later a synagogue with two cherubims surmounting it, was depicted. Others were made with a spring door imitating the entrance to a temple and were used, during the wedding feast, as containers of myrtle, perfume, incense or a relic. The myrtle symbolizes affection and duty.

The wedding ring was usually worn on the fourth finger of the right hand.

Gimmal Rings

The Gimmal rings were used by the Romans as pledge rings. They were usually made with two hoops (from the Latin *gemullus* "twin-born"), fitted together. Sometimes however, there were three hoops; one being given to each of the betrothed, and the third held by a maiden companion of the future bride. The three hoops were reunited and given back to the bride at the marriage ceremony.

Gemel or Gimmal rings were used at betrothals in England and in France as far back as the sixteenth century. Engagement or wedding rings with clasped hands as well as with other symbolical designs are still used in France, especially in Normandy. These rings are handed down as heirlooms from generation to generation.

Herrick notes the use of gimmal rings in "Hesperides":

"Thou sent'st me a true love knot, but I
  Returned a ring of jummals to imply
  Thy love had one knot, mine a triply tye."

MOTTOS AND "POESY RINGS"

During the fourteenth and fifteenth centuries, short, poetic verses or couplets known as "posies" (poesies) were usually inscribed on the outside of the plain rings used at betrothals. Later, these posies were inscribed on the inside of the rings. When a fiancé sent one to his beloved, a little bunch of flowers accompanied the sentimental token; as this was considerably smaller than the usual bouquet, it was called a nosegay. Although the custom of presenting poetically inscribed rings gradually died out, the sentimental practice of giving flowers continued. However, posy rings are still made use of by some of the peasants of France.

Rings inscribed with mottos, and given to insure the wearer good luck; or those worn as pledges, have been in use from the earliest times. Inscribed rings were used for religious, political and sentimental purposes by the Greeks and Romans and have been found inscribed with such words as ZHCAIC, XAIPE, KAAH, or votis meis Claudia vivas. The oldest rings with the name and title of the owners, are those found in the tombs of Egypt and date from the XVIIIth to the XXth Dynasty.

There are in the British Museum several "posy" rings that were used at betrothals during the sixteenth and seventeenth centuries. The following is a list of pretty "posies" collected by George Frederick Kunz and used in his book entitled "Rings". Some are in old French and others in Old English and Latin:

>Till death divide.
>Nemo nisi mors.
>(No one but Death.)
>Tout pour bein feyre.
>(In good faith.)
>Sans mal desyr
>(Without evil wish.)
>Amor vincit om
>(Love conquers all things.)
>Semper amenus
>(May we love forever.)
>Honeur et joye
>(Honour and joy.)
>Mon coeur avez
>(You have my heart.)
>Deux corps une coeur
>(Two bodies and one heart.)

Love him who gave thee this ring of gold,
'Tis he must kiss thee when thou art old.

This circle, though but small about,
The devil, jealousy, will keep out.

A virtuous wife doth banish strife.

Constancy and heaven are round,
And in this the emblem's found.

Eye doth find, heart doth choose,
Faith doth bind, death doth loose.

My love is fixed; I will not range,
I like my choice too well to change.

CIRCLETS OR HOOPS USED AT BETROTHALS

It has long been the common belief that anything round signifies eternal. To join the hands through a natural ring of stone meant a pledge. A round object was deemed so important at weddings that in many cases where a bridegroom was unable to provide a ring for his bride, a bracelet, a curtain ring, or even the Church key ring was used. That custom prevailed in Iceland and the Orkney Islands north of Scotland as late as the eighteenth century.

Wedding-Rings Worn on the Thumb

In England, about the middle of the seventeenth century, wedding rings were sometimes worn on the thumb. At the marriage ceremony, the ring was placed on the fourth finger of the left hand as usual, but the fashion for wedding rings of an extraordinary size compelled the wearers to transfer them to the thumb. This custom prevailed during the reign of George I but, as the rings diminished in size, the custom became obsolete.

Wedding-Rings for Men

In Germany, the bride and bridegroom exchange rings at the wedding ceremony. This is called "Trauringe", trust ring. The custom for a married man to wear a ring is observed in the Scandinavian and Teutonic countries as well as in some parts of England and France. At one time nearly all married Englishmen wore wedding-rings.

It was said that when a single man or woman was about to be married, a ring was to be worn on the index finger of the left hand and when married, on the third finger; the desire to remain single was indicated by a ring worn on the little finger.

Regard Rings

The custom of giving "Regard Rings" is a comparatively recent one, but it did not find much favor with the public. These rings were set with different stones; the first letter of each stone-name spelling the word "regard" (reading down) or the Christian name of the lady to whom it was given.

The following examples show how it was done:

R uby	*S* apphire
E merald	*O* pal
G arnet	*P* earl
A methyst	*H* yalite
R uby	*I* olite
D iamond	*A* methyst

RELIGIOUS DEDICATION OF VARIOUS FINGER JOINTS

The significance of the religious dedication of the finger-joints is taken from Kunz's book on Rings: "The upper joint of the thumb of the right hand was dedicated to God, the lower joint to the Virgin; the first joint of the index to St. Barnabas, the second to St. John, the third to St. Paul; the first joint of the middle finger to St. Simon Cleophas, the second to St. Thaddaeus, the third to St. Joseph; the first of the annular to St. Zacchaeus, the second to St. Stephen, the third to St. Luke; the first joint of the little finger to St. Leatus, the second to St. Mark, the third to St. Niccodemus. The dedication of the left hand fingers were: first joint of the thumb, to Christ, second joint to the Virgin; first joint of the index to St. James, the second to St. John the Evangelist, the third to St. Peter; first joint of the middle finger to St. Simon, the second to St. Matthew, the third to St. James the Greater; first joint of the annular to St. Jude, the second to St. Bartholomew, the third to St. Andrew; first joint of the little finger to St. Matthias, the second to St. Thomas, the third to St. Philip."

BIRTHSTONES, METAL, GEMS, THEIR SYMBOLS AND SUPERSTITIONS

January—Garnet
February—Amethyst
March—Bloodstone
April—Diamond
May—Emerald
June—Agate

July—Ruby
August—Sardonyx
September—Sapphire
October—Opal
November—Topaz
December—Turquoise

Gold has been called the metal of the sun or of man. *Silver* the metal of the moon; *Platinum* is the metal of Heaven; *Aluminum*, the metal of earth has no symbolic value for rings.

Diamond—It was formerly believed that a diamond in an engagement or wedding ring would inevitably bring bad luck to the wearer and her husband, because the interruption of the circle destroyed the love which would otherwise have been eternal. It became the favorite stone for an engagement ring, however, because of the belief that its sparkle was the fire of love. The Italian of the Medieval period called it *pietra* della reconciliazione, which means *peace between husband and wife.*

Amethyst—The Greeks believed that the amethyst was a charm against drunkenness. The Jews thought that the stone induced dreams and the name is derived from an Hebrew root.

Emerald—The emerald is supposed to protect and is the emblem of virtue. The Romans believed it to be symbolical of womanhood and nearly always had their rings set with one or more of these stones.

Amber—Amber is worn as an amulet and is supposed to change color with the health of the wearer, acting as a barometer of one's physical condition.

Coral—Coral also has healing charm, and during Medieval times was considered a protection against evil powers; "to hang coral about an infant's neck will save it from falls and sickness."

Sapphire—It is believed that the sapphire is a safeguard against misery and is lucky when worn as an amulet.

Opal—Until the eighteenth century opals were considered the luckiest of stones. Not only were they worn as charms to protect the wearer, but supernatural powers were attributed to them. But Sir Walter Scott's bit of superstitious fiction in his book "Anne of Geierstein" made opals the most dreaded of gems; and even to-day they are very unpopular in Europe and in America.

Ruby—Among the Romans, the ruby symbolized masculinity, and rings set with rubies were worn by men.

Pearls—It is a common belief among people in various countries that pearls are unlucky. In Oriental countries, however, they are considered to possess health-giving powers and to be able to impart a beautiful complexion to the wearer. In ancient Rome and Greece, pearls were looked upon as favorable in securing the good graces of the goddess Venus, because she wore them in preference to any other jewel. Among many of the German peasants, a bride will not wear pearls unless they have been placed in a tiny casket called gegen thranen, otherwise she believes that they would cause tears, provoked by the husband.

Turquoise—In the Orient the turquoise is considered a very lucky gem, and the wearer usually has the name of Allah or a verse from the Koran delicately carved into the stone to make the good fortune more auspicious. In Germany, the turquoise still is the favorite stone.

The present style of wedding rings in Europe and in America, is to have orange blossoms or wedding bells engraved on a narrow gold or platinum ring. The brides who are sentimentally inclined have their grandmothers' rings fashioned into ones of modern design. Gold is not much in favor with brides of to-day, but when covered with platinum or white gold, the family heirlooms comply with fashion and sentiment.

MARRIAGE CUSTOMS OF CUTTING AND SHAVING THE HAIR

Cutting the hair or shaving the eyebrows is no longer a marriage formality among nations, but the latter custom was still observed in Japan until some years ago. The Japanese bride shaved her eyebrows because they were considered her greatest charm and were removed at marriage to make her less attractive, and therefore, not a temptation to other men. Sometimes the brides blackened their teeth and cut their hair as well. The custom is rarely observed to-day. Among the Japanese, ancient Egyptians, ancient Britons and Jews, the symbolic significance of cutting the bride's hair, after the marriage ceremony, was to give further proof of her submission to her husband.

In Rome, boys who had reached the age of puberty, had their hair cut and a lock of it was burnt in honor of Apollo, the god of youth and manly beauty. The bulla, a little locket of gold which boys and girls wore round their necks, was also offered to Hercules, demi-god of strength and endurance. The girls offered their dolls to Venus, the goddess of love, and their gold lockets to Juno, the goddess of womanhood.

Most women of the Caucasus in Russia cut off their luxuriant hair to wear the platoke. This is a turban made of wool or linen and is rolled round their heads to indicate that they are married women. It is a gift of the bridegroom to the bride.

While cutting her hair, a bride will sing sad traditional lines such as "oh, my curls, my fair golden curls! Not for one nor two years have I arranged you! Every Saturday you were bathed, every Sunday you were ornamented and to-day, in a single hour, I must lose you!" After the hair is cut, an elderly woman rolls the cloth round the bride's head saying as she does so: "I cover your head with the platoke, my sister, and wish you health and happiness. Be pure as water, and fruitful as the earth." This constitutes the marriage ceremony; the bridegroom then escorts his bride through the village to show every one the transformation of the maiden's costume into that of a married woman.

Shaving at marriages, says l'Abbé Dubois, is the custom in several of the southern provinces of India. The natives have all the hair on their bodies shaved, with the exception of the eyebrows; this custom is observed by the Brahmins on marriage days and other solemn ceremonials. This custom of shaving the hair from the body to exemplify purity is not peculiar to the Brahmins; it was also common amongst the Jews, and was part of their ceremonial law (Numbers viii, 6, 7). Among the Orthodox Jews, married women can still be seen wearing wigs on their shaved heads. This is undoubtedly done to lessen their beauty according to the "Covenant of Hair" which compelled the shaving of the head, upon the making of a vow.

Among the Sutra tribes of India, a widow's head is shaved once a month. In other tribes, any child of ten or twelve who loses her husband in death is compelled to have her head shaved, though she may never have lived with him as his wife. An Indian widow of British Columbia had her hair cut at the death of her husband and could not remarry until her hair was fully grown. In the Upper Congo, it is the widower who shaves his head, often only in spots.

BANNS

In England, the publication of the banns previous to the marriage, dates back to the twelfth century and was "the first canonical enactment of the British Church contained in the eleventh canon of the Synod of Westminster, in London." It was either necessary to have the banns published three times before marriage could be contracted, or to have a special dispensation granted by the bishop. During the Commonwealth (1649-1660), banns were not only published in churches, but they could be announced publicly by a crier on market-days at the market nearest to the house of the contracting parties. If the couple was under twenty-one years of age, the marriage was "null and void" unless the publication was made with the parents' consent.

The origin of the publication of the banns antedates the enactment of the English canonical law; since the publication of the banns was the custom in France during the ninth century and Odo, bishop of Paris, made it compulsory in 1176. From other sources we gather that the custom of banns has evolved from the practice of knights called to take part in tournaments, and who were compelled to place their shields in a church near their dwelling. If they were accepted for the tournament, their names remained and others were warned off. This custom was deemed so important as to be practiced in betrothals.

The publication of the banns is compulsory in the Roman Catholic Church, or else a dispensation is demanded.

MARRIAGE AT THE CHURCH DOOR

"She was a worthy woman all her live,
Husbands at the church door, she had five."
The Wife of Bath (Chaucer)

In France (700 A.D.) there was a prescribed method for marrying and the nuptials consisted of two ceremonies. A priest, on arriving at the church door and finding there a couple wooing, asked them if they wanted to be properly married. There was an exchange of gifts and a benediction followed. Then the couple was asked to enter the church and to attend the Bride Mass. A hundred years later, priests would ask only for the couple's consent to marry, and if the gift had been given by the bridegroom to the bride, another one was requested by the priest to be given to the poor. Then the father or friend of the bride would give her away in marriage.

About the tenth century this form of marriage was practiced in England and the first part was the ceremony of the "gifta." It took place outside of the church door on the porch; the second ceremony was the Bride Mass which was performed in church.

A CURIOUS WEDDING CUSTOM IN KENT

In Kent there is a curious custom of strewing the pathway of a married couple leaving the church, not only with flowers, but with the emblems of the bridegroom's calling; carpenters walk on shavings; butchers on skins of slaughtered sheep; the followers of St. Crispin are honored with leather parings; paper-hangers with slips of papers; blacksmiths with old iron, rusty nails, etc. This custom was carried out in the ceremonies of all the lowlier professions.

HOLY ISLAND, OR LINDISFARNE

On the Holy Island, in the North Sea, two miles from the coast of Northumberland, another custom consists of making the bridal pair and their attendants leap over a stone placed in their path outside the church porch. This is called the "louping" or "petting" stone, and the bride must leave all her hobbies and humors behind her when she crosses it. This custom is also observed in the village of Belford as well as in the neighboring village of Embleton in Northumberland. In the latter place, however, the custom differs slightly. "Two stout young lads place a wooden bench across the door of the church porch, assist the bride, bridegroom, and her friends to surmount the obstacle, and then look out for a donation from the bridegroom." (Henderson, p. 38.)

In some villages, the newly married pair before entering their new home, is saluted twice by the shooting of three guns, after which the wedding cake and the plate containing it are thrown into the air. If the plate breaks, the fragments of it are considered lucky omens, and girls scramble for the pieces. The failure of the plate to break foretells an unhappy married life for both the bride and bridegroom.

BEST MAN AND BRIDEGROOM

In ancient times, when a man captured a girl for his wife, he invariably had to depend on the assistance of one friend at least, to help in the seizure of the future bride. This "best man" saw that no one interfered with the capture of the struggling maiden.

The rôle of the "best man" was eventually changed and the groomsmen became known as "bride knights" and waited on the bride instead. In the Roman confarreatio, the marriage ceremony of the patricians, it was the custom to have the bride accompanied by bachelors, known as "bride knights," to the Pontifex Maximus; but on her return home, married "bride knights" went before her in ceremonial fashion.

The bridegroom used to be called, "The groom of the bride"; it was customary, on the wedding day, for the bridegroom to wait on his bride at the table. In olden days, the bride gave gifts to the "bride knights"; but to-day, the bridegroom presents the "best man" or bride escorts, with a jewel or some other gift for the "giving of the bride", a survival of the custom of marriage by purchase.

The bachelor's dinner as it is observed to-day, originated in Sparta.

BRIDESMAIDS

In ancient Asia, as the marriage by capture became less savage, the maiden companions of the future bride would stand upon the threshold of her house and refuse to let the would-be-bridegroom and his friends enter. They showered the men with balls of boiled rice and would refuse them entrance until they were given gifts. The present tradition of the bridegroom's gifts to the bridesmaids is undoubtedly a survival thereof. The instruction of bridesmaids evolved from the Roman custom of having ten witnesses at weddings.

The custom of having the bridesmaids attired in costumes similar to that worn by the bride was observed by many nations. That was done in order to confuse the evil spirits who were eager to harm the marrying couple. The young friends of the bride were all dressed like the bride to mystify the spirits. The young escorts of the groom were also dressed like him for the same reason.

THE WEDDING DRESS

The color of the bridal gown varies in different countries; but white has been, from time immemorial, the emblem of the bride's purity, simplicity, candor, and innocence. The wearing of white was observed by the early Greeks, they believed that white was the emblem of joy. White flowers and flowing garments were the Greek's attire for feast days. They even painted their bodies white on the eve of their wedding ceremonies. The latter custom was also observed by the wild tribes of the ancient Patagonians in South America on their festive occasions. The ancient Romans wore white when a child was born.

The Japanese bride wears a white bridal gown and a golden girdle. Both gown and girdle are the bridegroom's gifts to the bride.

Yellow, green and black are the three colors which are unpopular among brides; when not using the customary white, blue is substituted. A wedding dress must never be dyed or remade as it is considered unlucky for the bride.

The following are just a few of the color schemes in use by brides in different countries:

Armenia—Various bright colors are combined.

China—Red is the most desirable color.

Norway—The superstitious bride and her bridesmaids wear green in preference to any other colors. Whenever the bride's wedding dress is of another color, the costumes of the bridesmaids remain green.

Persia—A large blue sheet is wrapped round the bride's body.

Roumania—A sleeveless jacket embroidered in red and gold is worn.

Spain—Black is worn by the peasants. White is worn by nearly all the brides of the upper classes.

Sweden—Usually a black or a dark colored costume trimmed with ribbons and flowers of all shades is mostly in use.

Switzerland—In parts of Switzerland, the bride as well as the guests wear black.

Tuscany—A black or dark dress is preferred.

THE BRIDAL VEIL

Some writers are of the opinion that the custom of wearing a veil at weddings, originated as a sign of submission, while others believe that it was the emblem of freedom. A few maintain that the bridal veil is a relic of the Purdah custom;

no one was ever to look upon the face of a woman until she was married. Women were secluded and covered from head to foot until their marriage day, when it was the privilege of the bridegroom to "lift the veil" and proclaim loudly his enthusiasm over the bride's beauty.

In Jerusalem, women have never appeared outside their homes with their heads uncovered. This custom of wearing a handkerchief called chalebi to avert the Schedim or Djinns, who are eager to get near the uncovered heads of women, had its origin in Arabia. The Djinns are the offspring of fire, taking the form of animals and human beings, and are able to make themselves visible or invisible at will. There are good and evil ones among them. They are able to assume the character of either beauty or ugliness, and are therefore terribly dreaded. The Chinese' sacred umbrella, which is held over the bride's head, is intended to prevent the evil spirits from reaching her. The veil at weddings, apparently originated from that superstition.

Through the East, a purdah-nashin literally means a woman who is hidden under a long veil. To "lift the purdah" is a popular expression used all over Europe, which means that a secret has been discovered. The custom is observed by the Egyptians, Arabs, Hindus, and many European and Asiatic peoples. At the marriage ceremony the bride in China, Burma, Korea, Russia, Bulgaria, Manchuria, and Persia is completely hidden under a veil. It is strange to note that in Western countries where there is no restriction on the bride being seen by her future husband, the custom of wearing a veil nevertheless prevails.

The evil eye superstition appears to have been the real cause of hiding women under the veil; for women, the embodiment of beauty and delicacy, are the especial desire of the evil one. The veil is supposed to ward off this influence.

Among Anglo-Saxons, it was the custom to have a "care-cloth" held over the bride and bridegroom by four men; but later it was held over the bride's head only. The square cloth, called chupeh among the ancient Jews, is still used to-day in the Jewish marriage ceremony in the form of a canopy held over the couple. In the Catholic churches of some countries, a canopy is still used during the marriage ceremony.

Grecian brides used to offer their veils to Hera, the goddess of marriage, to assure them of an easy childbirth. Among some of the French peasants of to-day, the bridal veil is put away immediately after the ceremony, to be used again only at her death.

Women have always been the ones who wore veils; but among a nomad tribe of the Touaregs, the custom is reversed, and the men wear them.

The Touareg boys begin to wear veils when only thirteen years of age, and they keep their faces hidden for the rest of their lives. During their meals, the mouth only is exposed.

ORANGE BLOSSOMS AS BRIDAL WREATHS

In the delightful legend of the Golden Fruit of Hesperides in Greek mythology, golden apples (now believed to have been oranges) were presented to Hera on her wedding night when she became the wife of Zeus. Thus she became the goddess of celestial phenomena, the genius of womanhood and guardian of the female sex. However, the custom of wearing a wreath of orange blossoms was introduced into Europe at the time of the Crusades.

There is an old Spanish legend which gives an interesting account of its inception. One of the Spanish kings had a specimen of a plant of which he was very proud; the French Ambassador was extremely desirous of obtaining an offshoot. The daughter of the king's gardener, to provide herself with the necessary dowry to enable her to marry her lover, sold the Frenchman the orange slip at a high price. To show her gratitude to the plant which had secured her happiness, she bound in her hair a wreath of its blossoms on her wedding day. This legend sufficiently establishes the antiquity of the custom, however, many years elapsed before it spread to other European countries.

The first orange-tree was introduced into France during the sixteenth century and the original tree still exists in the orange grove at Versailles. The custom of wearing orange blossoms at weddings spread to England from France about 1820.

In China, orange blossoms are believed to be lucky, and the white blossoms are the emblems of purity, chastity and innocence. The orange-tree is an evergreen, and it is the only tree which bears blossoms and fruit at the same time. That was the reason it was chosen in the East as the tree symbolic of fruitfulness. Its blossoms were worn by the bride to insure her against sterility.

Wreaths of corn or wheat, the emblem of fertility among the Anglo-Saxons, Greeks and Romans, were furnished by the churches, and temporarily loaned to the bride for the ceremony.

Orange blossoms are delicate and costly and can only be worn by the wealthy. Artificial blossoms worn at a wedding should be discarded before a month has elapsed, otherwise they are supposed to be unlucky for the bride.

CARRYING THE BRIDE OVER THE THRESHOLD

The tradition of carrying the bride over the threshold is a relic of primitive marriage by capture. It was observed by the Romans, as is evidenced in Becker's Gallus, where he says concerning the bride, "they do not allow her to step over the threshold of the house, but people sent forward, carry her over." Also carrying the bride over the threshold was done in order to prevent her tripping over the step, and in that way avoiding the bad omen. This custom was observed by the Arabs, the Turks, Persians and Kabyles of Africa; also by the Red Skin Indians of Canada, the Chinese, the Abyssinians, the English and the Austrians.

In some villages of Austria the bride and bridegroom drink wine and eat bread before entering their new home, throwing the empty glass over the roof. As they step over the threshold their hands must be tied together.

In Morea, one of the wedding guests breaks a pomegranate on the threshold as a sign of good luck. In Rhodes, Greece, the husband crushes the pomegranate with his foot as he passes the threshold, while the guests shower the bride with corn, cotton-seeds, and orange-water. This resembles the rice throwing ceremony, and it is done with the same motive.

In Cyprus, as a sign of good luck, the bridegroom sacrifices a fowl by cutting its head with an axe, an old custom which differs little from that of the Arabs, who sacrifice a sheep. The

Copts of Egypt and the Persians also sacrifice a sheep at the marriage ceremony, placing it across the threshold of the newly married couple's home, and the bride steps over it as she enters.

RICE THROWING

The custom of throwing rice at weddings is very old and many authorities differ as to its origin. It was observed by many as part of the marriage ceremony, and it was considered the emblem of fecundity and prosperity. One of the many ceremonies at a Hindu marriage consisted in the bride's father giving the bridegroom grains of red-colored rice with betel leaves. The bridegroom then threw three handsful of rice over the bride; and she responded in the same manner.

In many countries throughout the world, rice or any other grain is thrown after the couple. A Persian custom, before Talmudic times, was that of sowing barley in a flower-pot several days before a wedding. On the wedding day it was thrown over the couple's heads as an omen of fertility. Wheat, corn, and nuts had the same significance, and the pair was not only showered with them, but they were strewn in their path to assure the couple a large family and prosperity. At the birth of a son, a cedar was planted; at the birth of a girl, an acacia was planted. Before the wedding, a tree was felled and a part of the wood was used as an ornament during the wedding ceremony. At the same time, one of the guests led the bridal procession carrying a pair of fowls. These customs lasted until the Middle Ages.

The ancient Romans threw nuts and all kinds of sweets at the bride. This custom was eventually changed to confetti throwing and has spread throughout Europe and America. In Greece, as well as in Rome, a pomegranate was eaten by the bride on her wedding day. In Scotland, breaking an oat-cake over the head of the bride, has the same significance as rice throwing. In many parts of southern France, throwing fruit, especially figs, is a very popular custom among the peasants.

There has always been a superstition among the ancients, that at weddings, as well as at funerals, evil spirits were ever near; and that the throwing of rice was food for them, thus keeping them away from the bride and bridegroom. Among the Polynesians, Melanesians, Dyaks of Borneo, and many others, the eating of rice together, constitutes marriage.

SHOES AT WEDDINGS

Ages ago, the placing of a shoe on a tract of land was a symbol of ownership. To close a contract on a land purchase, the ancient Assyrians and Hebrews handed a sandal to the buyer. From these ancient traditions and practices, evolved the custom of throwing an old shoe after a bride; symbolizing the forfeiture of all right of dominion over their daughter by the parents. Among the early Anglo-Saxons, the father gave the bride's shoe to the future husband, who touched her on the head or on the nape of the neck with it, to show his authority. A bridegroom used to hang a slipper in a conspicuous place in his house for the same reason.

The exchange of sandals among the Egyptians was a sign of transferred property. Formerly, in Greece and in Rome, to express adoration it was the custom to remove the shoes when nearing a shrine. This custom is still observed by the Mohammedans, who, when entering a mosque, remove their slippers and leave them at the door, as a sign of respect. Loosening the shoe is a widely observed custom all through the East.

In Turkey, even to-day, the bridegroom, after the marriage ceremony, is followed by wedding guests and pelted with slippers, by way of adieu.

In Germany, the bride throws her shoe to the wedding guests. This has the same significance as the custom of throwing the garter or stocking; while in France, as throughout the world to-day, the wedding bouquet itself is thrown.

Among the ancient Northmen, when a man adopted a son, the boy put on the shoes of the foster parent. In Egypt, a slave used to walk behind his master carrying his shoe.

In many countries, it is believed that leather will keep the evil spirits away. In Scotland and in Ireland, old shoes were not thrown exclusively at weddings; superstitious persons used to throw shoes at anyone who started on a new venture by way of wishing him success. In India, an old shoe turned upside down on the roof of a new home would assure the married couple prosperity, and keep away evil influences.

Shoes at one time were an essential part of the bride's gifts. In fact, in Hamburg and in Transylvania, it was the law for the bridegroom to give the bride a pair of new shoes. On the wedding day, in Greece, the "best man" was obliged to put a new pair of shoes on the bride.

Authorities differ as to the origin of the throwing of old shoes at weddings, but whatever the origin may be, the real significance of the custom has always been associated with power, ownership and good luck. A humorist once said, that "the throwing of old slippers indicated that the chances of matrimony are slippery."

WEDDING CAKE CUSTOMS

The function of bride and bridegroom jointly

partaking of a repast has always been the most essential part of the wedding ceremony. It still exists to-day in the form of our modern wedding breakfast. In many cases, pieces of the wedding cake are previously packed in tiny boxes for the bridesmaids to take home. The wedding-cake custom of to-day, requires that the bride should be the first one to cut the cake if she wishes to be happily married, and then the bridesmaids each take a piece. The popular superstition in England and in France is to pass a morsel through the wedding-ring, place it in the left stocking, and then place the cake under the pillow. The future husband will appear in a dream that night.

In Rome, the marriage of a young couple of a patrician family was called confarreatio, or the ceremony of the wedding-cake. In the presence of ten witnesses, the bride and bridegroom partook of a piece of cake made of salt and water. It was believed that children who were born of such a union were eligible for high, sacred honors. The word confarreatio means eating together. After the married couple had eaten of the cake, each of the guests took a piece of the cake for good luck. Our present wedding-cake custom is the survival of the Roman confarreatio.

The importance of the wedding-cake in Greece was so pronounced that an extraordinary amount of time, thought, and energy was spent in baking it. Several days were devoted to making the cake amidst endless ceremonies. The first two days, the bride and her women friends sifted and carried the grain to the mill. The third day they brought home the flour from the mill, and more friends came to the house to help knead the dough. The kneading ceremony was a curious one. At one end of the trough, a little boy sat with a sword, and at the other end, a little girl threw coins into the dough. The wedding ring was also thrown in by the little girl at a moment when no one was supposed to be looking. The children chosen for this ceremony had to be those who had never lost any near relative, because that would have brought ill luck to the bride and bridegroom. This quaint cake ceremony was of a symbolic nature: the boy represented the future husband whose duty was to protect the wife, and the little girl personified the wife who had charge of the domestic duties.

After the cake was baked, friends partook of it, and each one hoped to find the wedding ring. Whoever found it returned it to the bridegroom in exchange for a gift; and the fortunate finder was then looked upon as the next bride or bridegroom. That same afternoon, the remainder of the cake was placed over a bowl of water and the young couple danced around it three times, all the while singing the "Song of the Wedding-Cake." When this dance was over, the cake was broken into pieces, and the bride and bridegroom were showered with the fragments. This signified that the guests and friends wished for the future prosperity of the couple.

The following are a few of the many ceremonies performed at marriages in various countries, and the kinds of food and drink used:

Anglo-Saxons—Small cakes were given to each guest to take home.

American Indians—(Iroquois, Navajos and others) A cake was made by the bride and presented by her to the bridegroom.

Britons (ancient)—A married couple drank "marriage-mead" for a whole month.

Brittany—Bread soaked in brandy is eaten by the couple.

Brazil—The bride and bridegroom drink native brandy.

China—A Chinese couple drinks tea.

England—The modern word "bridal" was originally written "byrd-eale," meaning "bride-ale," which was served at the marriage feast.

Greece—A wedding-cake made of sesame seed and honey and part of a quince had to be eaten by the bride to signify that she was willing to marry for "better or for worse." Sweet and bitter food symbolized the good and bad of married life.

Hovas (Madagascar)—Eating together constitutes the marriage ceremony. This custom is also observed by most of the primitives living on the islands of the Pacific Ocean.

India—The bride and bridegroom must eat the betel nut together; this custom is universal among the Hindus.

Italy—A "matrimonial-cake" made of sugared almond is eaten by the bride and groom and pieces of it are sent to their friends.

Jews—At a Jewish ceremony consecrated wine is given to the married pair.

Germany—The married pair must partake of soup from the same plate.

Japan—A Japanese couple is compelled to drink several cups of saki (wine) as part of the marriage ceremony.

Russia—A Russian bride believes that if she tastes the wedding-cake before the marriage ceremony, she will lose her husband's love. After the wedding ceremony, while still wearing a crown of flowers and ribbons, the bride offers a loaf of bread decorated with colored ribbons to each guest.

Scandinavia—The contracting parties must drink from the same goblet to seal their union.

Scotland—A cake was broken on the bride's

head and the pieces were kept by her during her married life. On the anniversaries of the marriage, the husband and wife ate a small piece of the cake for good fortune and long life.

Turkey—Sweetmeats were eaten by the bride and bridegroom from "lip to lip."

HONEYMOON

The word "honeymoon" originated with the ancient Teutons. It signifies the drinking of mead for forty days after the marriage. This is a beverage made from honey. Attila, the celebrated king of the Huns, who boasted of the appellation, "The Scourge of God," is said to have died on his nuptial night from an uncommon effusion of blood, brought on by indulging too freely in this beverage, at his wedding feast.

Formerly, a month was spent by the couple in hiding from the angry father of the captured bride. The honeymoon or the "month away from home" custom, may be a relic from the marriage by capture among the primitive people. When the couple returned home they always brought back gifts to subdue the father's wrath. Also, when a couple eloped because they loved each other, they stayed away for a month enjoying what we call a honeymoon.

In many countries, it was customary to keep

the newly married pair secluded for a certain number of days. In Java, the period of seclusion lasts forty days. This is an enforced honeymoon. But the most curious custom is that the bride and bridegroom hide before they are married and are not allowed to see anyone nor to do any work.

"Hyblean bliss," a term frequently used by poets, means "honeyed bliss". Hybla is a town in Sicily famous for its honey.

Mead, metheglin, and hydromel were three different kinds of drinks made from honey; there were from twenty to forty varieties of mead which could be made with a compound of spices, sweet herbs, honey and water. Hydromel was a mixtures of cloves, ginger, rosemary, honey and water, fermented with ale yeast. Eliezar Edwards in his book of "Words, Facts and Phrases" gives the following recipe:

"After the honey had been drained from the comb, the latter was scalded to dissolve any honey that might still adhere. The wax being strained away, the sweetened liquor was strengthened by additional honey until a fresh egg floating in it would show a disc the size of half a crown. This was the test for strength. The liquor was then put into casks with a little yeast, and when fermentation was over, it was corked up."

The belief in lucky and unlucky days and months in many countries varies greatly. The Romans and the Greeks did not think May or the early part of June a propitious time to marry, though if it was a new moon or a full moon the marriage could take place. It was believed that a marriage in May would bring bad luck to the couple during the year and that all their children would be born sickly.

The Hindus marry during the months of March, April, May, and June; the two latter being those most favored. It was not superstition which prompted them to marry during those months. The time was more favorable; their work was suspended because of the extreme heat; the harvests being over, the money from their agricultural labors helped them to defray the expenses of their elaborate and costly marriage ceremonies.

During the other months, it was very difficult to find a day with auspicious signs, for The Zodiac complicated these weddings and made it almost impossible for them to take place.

In Italy, June is preferred by brides. Among the peasants, the marriage ceremony is usually performed on a Sunday. This custom is said to be observed because the Italian woman believes that, if she were married on Monday, all her children would be girls, and idiots; if on Tuesday, the first born would be a faun or have a club foot; Thursday is the day of the Witches and the three Furies; Wednesday and Friday are feast days; so Sunday remains for a wedding. Widows, however, may marry on a Saturday without incurring any ill omens.

The Chinese have special days for marrying which are recorded in their almanacs. September is a bad month, but marriages in the Spring months or in December are considered very propitious.

Friday is a very favorable day among the Bedouins of Mount Sinai and the Mohammedan negroes of Senegambia. Danes prefer Thursday, Saturday or Sunday in July or December. In Wales, those who still believe in fairies never marry on Friday. The Copts usually marry on a Saturday.

The custom of marrying during the crescent of the moon or when it is full, is observed in Thuringia, Orkney, Esthonia, India, Greece and Germany. In the latter country Tuesday and Saturday are the lucky days.

In Scotland, May is an unlucky month. Couples delight in getting married on the first of January, in the belief that it is good to start anything new on the beginning of the New Year.

Among the Catholic peoples; April is the favored month, because Lent is over. May is still considered unlucky by many; and June, August, September, December and January are popular months for weddings. Many Catholics still believe in the proverbs: "Married in Lent, you'll live to repent," and "Choose not alone a proper mate, but a proper time to marry." In Brussels, the marriage day is chosen according to the social standing of the couple; wealthy people marry on Tuesday; the middle classes on Wednesday at eleven in the morning; and Saturday is the day for the lower classes as they may be married without a fee on that day.

In France, there are many superstitions attached to the day or month chosen for weddings. One of the most curious customs still observed in Burgundy by the peasant maidens, is to place their hands out of the window at midnight of the last day of February and while listening to the strokes of the clock chant very low:

> "Bonjour, Mars: comment te portes-tu Mars?
> (Good morning, March: how art thou, March?
>
> Montre moi dans mon dormant, celui que j'aimerai
> Show me while I sleep whom I shall love
> > dans mon vivant."
> > when awake.)

Then they retire believing their future husbands will appear in their dreams.

In Switzerland, particularly in Lucerne, any Monday in February is the most propitious day for marrying.

To be married on the bridegroom's birthday is very fortunate for the couple, but especially so for the bride; but if the day happens to be on the thirteenth it should be avoided. The bride should never be married on her birthday.

The following tables stipulate the wedding days which superstition has decreed to be either lucky or unlucky:

LUCKY DAYS

January	2	4	11	19	21	
February	1	3	10	19	21	
March	3	5	12	20	23	
April	2	4	12	20	22	
May	2	4	12	20	23	
June	1	3	11	19	21	
July	1	3	12	21	31	
August	2	11	18	20	30	
September	1	16	18	19	28	
October	1	8	15	17	27	29
November	5	11	13	22	25	
December	8	10	19	23	29	

UNLUCKY DAYS

January	1	3	7	10	12
February	2	4			
March	1	6	8		
April	6	11			
May	5	6	7		
June	7	15			
July	5	19			
August	12	17			
September	6	17			
October	6				
November	15	19			
December	15	16	17		

The most unlucky days of all are the second of February, second of June, second of November and the first of December.

WEDDING SUPERSTITIONS IN MANY LANDS

Superstitions will never entirely disappear. They are the efforts of the uneducated to explain the occult, to probe unprecedented occurrences, or to forecast future events. Mysteries are the bane of humankind; men demand solution to all problems, rational or spiritual. The following are a few old superstitions to which many nations still cling:

Bavaria—Among the peasants of Bavaria, a young man about to propose marriage believes that in order to be happily married, he must present the future bride with an uneven number of coins.

A betrothed maiden should keep at a distance from a dead or dying person if she wants to be happy in marriage. Finding something in her path, she should pass it by, careful not to step upon it.

Belgium—At a Belgian wedding the bridesmaids collect money from the guests, and the coins are thrown to the poor at the church door.

Bohemia—On her return from church, a bride who still believes in the "marriage devil" is given a glass by her mother-in-law. The glass is filled, and, after partaking of its contents, the bride throws it over her shoulder. The breaking of the glass is an ill omen, but, if it remains whole, it signifies good fortune for the bride and groom.

England—In olden days, an uneven number of guests was considered unlucky, and forecasted the early death of one of the company.

Yorkshire—In Yorkshire, and in many parts of South Ireland, there was prevalent a custom of borrowing a wedding ring for good luck. In Ireland, when a bridegroom could not afford to buy a wedding ring, he would hire one and return it after the ceremony.

Sussex—In Sussex, the bridesmaids who wished to marry during the same year, robbed the bride of every pin, on her return from the wedding ceremony. In many parts of England, a bride never used any of the pins she wore on her wedding day; neither were the bridesmaids supposed to use them, as that would deprive the bride of some happiness in her married life.

The belief prevails that the bridegroom should never see the wedding costume before he sees his bride in it at the altar. A bridegroom must not give the bride pearls on her wedding day. The bride and bridegroom must also avoid seeing each other before they meet at church.

It used to be the custom upon the marriage of a younger sister for the elder sister to dance barefoot. It was thus she avoided the dread of spinsterhood. Sometimes this dance was performed in green stockings in order to hasten the wedding.

A wedding ring should never be removed from the finger. English peasants think that it is very unlucky to stumble on the wedding day.

Derbyshire—It was customary at Hope Church, in Derbyshire, on the publication of the banns, as well as at the solemnization of the marriage, for the clerk to call out loudly, "God speed you well!" which was pronounced in the Derbyshire dialect, "God speed you weel!"

In some parts of Derbyshire, the custom of warning the bees of the coming of a wedding was intended to avoid unpleasant future events in the married life of the couple. Ribbons were used to decorate the hives, and the announcement was sung to the bees by the bride and bridegroom, their relatives and friends.

The bride and bridegroom are compelled to walk very closely together on their way to church to prevent the witches from getting between them and neither must they look around. The one first rising from the altar is expected to be the first to die.

Norfolk and Suffolk—Among the fishermen of Norfolk and Suffolk, a wedding never took place unless it was during high tide. This was supposed to bring happiness and prosperity to the future pair.

Wales—The superstitious people of Wales believed three lights burning on the same table forecasted an unexpected marriage.

Germany—If a bride steps on the bridegroom's foot at the altar during the wedding ceremony, she believes that she will dominate her husband. A cat's sneeze is a good omen. A dog's howl is a bad one.

Prussia and Thuringia—Dishes broken at the threshold of a marrying pair bring good fortune. Before the marriage ceremony, a bride will put salt in her pockets to keep away the evil spirits. In her shoes, she carries hairs of different cattle; this will cause their own herds to increase and bring prosperity. At the feast, bride and bridegroom eat soup out of the same dish. The last spoonful is avoided, however, because death lurks within it.

Going to church, the bridegroom never looks back to avoid the accusation of looking for another bride. Meeting a priest on his way to administer the Holy Sacrament signifies the early death of either the bride or groom. The sneeze of a priest during the marriage ceremony is considered an evil omen.

One of the strangest superstitions observed by most of the German peasants and especially those living in the Black Forest, is the arrangement of the articles in the dowry-cart. In the bed cover which is part of her trousseau, five crosses are carefully sewn to subdue the witches who are very angry and vicious on that day. In order to be assured of a painless childbirth, the spinning-wheel is so placed as to have its side facing the horses who pull the cart. When the dowry-cart arrives at the bridegroom's house, his duty is to mark every article for the household with consecrated chalk, and holy water is sprinkled over everything in the cart. The woman carries a crucifix with her believing that she will save her husband from trouble during their married life. In some parts of Germany, mainly in Hanover, the breaking of dishes at the departure of the bride brings good luck.

Greece—In ancient Greece a game of divination was played, called "alectrymance", or "divination by the cock or hen." A circle was traced on the ground, and was divided into twenty-four parts. Grains of corn were so arranged in each compartment to represent the alphabet. A cock was then let in and the first grain of corn picked indicated the first letter of the name of the future husband.

Many of the peasants of Greece are extremely superstitious and still believe in the existence of a vampire and an evil eye; all kinds of customs are observed to forestall them. Coins are sewn in the mattress of the bed of a newly married pair for good luck.

In Greece, a bride lets a coin drop from her lips into a well, then draws water from it. She pours this water on the bridegroom's hands. This is supposed to give him everlasting strength to provide for his wife and his future family and assures them of prosperity and a long life together.

India—The Hindus have implicit faith in their innumerable good and bad omens, and the success of their marriage literally depends on what happens before, during, and immediately after the ceremony. When a Hindu father is on his way to negotiate a bride for his son and he sees some ill-omened animal crossing his path, he returns home without accomplishing his purpose. But if everything goes well, he makes known the object of his visit. Then the girl's father must face south and wait for a weird cry from the lizards who dwell in the house. It is only then that he accepts the future son-in-law and the gift that seals the bargain.

A wedding never takes place during a rainstorm, and a full moon is propitious for a marriage.

If a Hindu kills a frog, a marriage is forecast; and in Bengal, if a butterfly flutters near a person, his marriage is assured.

A maiden who wishes to marry, gazes at the bridegroom during a wedding ceremony, and leaves at once. The Hindus place a great deal of faith in leather and at their weddings use old shoes and skins for the decorations.

Italy—In many parts of Italy, a bridegroom will avoid the publication of the banns made when the moon is declining; nor will he be present in church if they are announced at that time, believing that his children would be either crippled or mute at birth.

There are many superstitions about the wedding ring among the peasants of Italy. Losing the ring prognosticates early death for the bride, while dropping it accidentally on the ground, is a sign of ill-luck for both the bride and bridegroom. The wedding ring is believed to have many curative properties. A sty will disappear forthwith when touched with it. In Spain, it is believed that the water into which a wedding ring has been dropped will cure sore eyes.

When there are several unmarried sisters in a family, the first one to marry is expected to spill hot water in front of the house. The unmarried sister who will first touch the dampened soil will be the next bride. In presenting gifts to one another, the bride and bridegroom must choose carefully, so as not to come in contact with any objects such as scissors or combs which are the favorite articles of witches, and therefore of ill omen.

There is a universal superstition attached to the birth of boy twins. The first born is supposed to be the child of love, and the second the child of lightning. The latter child is said to be favored by fate and good fortune is ever at his heels. This superstition is very popular throughout Italy.

In Corsica, marriage between blood relatives is considered a most desirable union.

Japan—A young Japanese maiden would never be induced to pour tea over a bowl of "red rice," because in doing so, she causes rain on her wedding day, which is considered very unlucky. Neither will a bride or bridegroom wear purple at the wedding ceremony for fear that their "marriage-tie" might loosen, since purple is supposed to be the color which fades fastest.

The emblem of marriage in Japan is the orange-tree specially decorated for the occasion. The embellishments consist of a fabulous beast which is supposed to represent "the wise men," also a goose and a gander, and many fans of delicate hues and designs. If the bride meets a Shinto priest, it is considered a good omen. The bride believes that if she can secure flowers for her wedding bouquet which a maiden has plucked in the snow, they will bring her happiness. The Japanese symbol of marriage is a girdle. There is a similarity between marriage emblems of Japan and those of China.

Lovers' Superstitions — Young men and women of Italy who are eager to know whom they will marry, obtain a stone from a neighboring cemetery at midnight, and place it under their pillows while they sleep; this stone is capable of revealing the identity of their future mate.

In Italy as well as in some parts of France, on All Saints' Day, the unbroken peel of an apple thrown over the left shoulder will reveal the lover's name.

When an Irish maiden wishes to find out whether her lover is true to her, she eats the white of a hard-boiled egg, highly salted. She must go to bed without drinking anything or speaking to anyone. If in her dreams her lover offers her a drink, she is convinced that he is untrue.

Whenever a bent sixpence is found by an Irishman it is unlucky. If however, he finds a coin cut in two and gives one part of it to his lady, their faithfulness will last as long as they each keep half of the coin.

The custom of wearing

"Something old and something new,
 Something borrowed and something blue,"

was an ancient practice among the Israelites. Blue was worn as a sign of love, purity, and fidelity.

This custom is observed to the present day.

Many superstitions are attached to sneezing. It is commonly believed that to sneeze on Sunday before breaking a fast, is a sign that one will meet one's lover within the week.

It is also believed that a sneeze on Saturday, brings a sweetheart on Sunday.

Being photographed together or exchanging photographs before marriage is considered unlucky.

Addressing each other as husband and wife before being married often leads to no marriage at all.

A popular superstition among women is:

"Thrice a bridesmaid, never a bride, but luck will change after the seventh time."

Persia—In some parts of Persia, a bride's hair is shaved at the neck because of an old superstition that a special hair called the "Angel of Death" grows here and will bring ill-luck if not removed. Her hands and feet are stained for this ceremony.

After the marriage ceremony, the bride arrives home at the head of a procession, riding on a mule harnessed with bells. The first things taken into her new home are bread, cheese, and salt, harbingers of prosperity.

Russia—Russian peasants are very superstitious about marriage. They believe that the happiness of the future couple depends upon the submerging of their parents in water or by rolling them in snow.

Scandinavia—In many parts of Scandinavia, especially in Sweden, the shirt made by the bride and given to the bridegroom may only be worn on the wedding day. Then it is hidden until the day of his burial. Knives, shoes, or handkerchiefs are never to be presented to the bride or bridegroom. It is believed that the knives would sever their love; the shoes would cause the unfaithfulness of the husband; and the handkerchiefs would wipe out their affections.

In Sweden there is a proverb which says that when a man shares bread with a young girl it is the beginning of their love.

A bride in Sweden, will rejoice if it rains or snows on her wedding day because it is a good omen. She must wear shoes without any ornament, in order to have an easy childbirth. The bride's father places a silver coin in her left shoe to insure her future prosperity. If she tears any article worn on her wedding day, she will suffer ill-treatment from her husband. In order to dominate him she must make the first purchase, so she usually buys a pin from her bridesmaid.

In Denmark, the bride and bridegroom go to church in separate processions, each being last in line. The bride must only look forward to avoid an unhappy life.

Scotland—No green is ever worn at weddings among the Lowland Scotch people, because it is the color believed to be used by the fairies, and is an omen of revenge. Many still believe that green vegetables should not be eaten at the feast. The wearing of feathers at a marriage or during a honeymoon is very unlucky.

If a caged bird died, or if a bride accidentally broke a dish, it was a prognostication of ill omen. If a bride left the house on her wedding day before the ceremony, she had to pull up her skirts to avoid ill-luck. On her way to church she always gave a coin to the first person she met. If she encountered a horse or a funeral procession on the way, it was a good omen.

Many Highlanders are kept in constant fear at weddings because they are superstitious and still believe in evil spirits. The bridegroom used to leave his shoes outside his bedroom on the eve of his wedding for good luck.

After a Scotch marriage ceremony the bride's clothes are put away until the day of her burial. Salt is the first thing used by the married couple in the new household. A great quantity of it is sprinkled on the floors to protect themselves against the evil eye.

The Irish are superstitious about birds. They

never kill robins because they had their breasts stained red at the Cross of Christ. This superstition is also believed by the Catholic French peasants.

Robert Lynd in "Home Life in Ireland" gives the following Irish rhyme about the magpies:

> "One for sorrow,
>   Two for joy,
>   Three for a marriage,
>   Four for a boy."

He further writes that "it is unlucky to meet a priest or a red-haired person when one is setting out on a journey."

"God forgive you, father, you've spoilt my day for me," said a holiday-making girl to a priest she met on the road.

"God forgive you, Bridget, for your foolish superstitions," replied the priest. A red-haired person is also an ill-omen when seen at a wedding.

Switzerland—If tapers are accidentally extinguished or fail to burn, it is considered very unfavorable for the future couple.

The gelbe-frau, mistress of ceremonies at a Swiss wedding, removes the wreath of flowers from the bride's head and sets fire to it with a taper. If the wreath burns quickly it is a good omen; but if it smoulders, unhappiness will be the bride's fate. The bride then kneels over the ashes and prays for the heavenly blessing.

Tyrol—To conclude the betrothal ceremony, wine is drunk by the couple. Spilling the wine is a bad omen; and the superstitious Tyrolese have a proverb which is supposed to account for the unhappiness of a married pair: "they have spilt the wine between them."

GENERAL SUPERSTITIONS

"Never try on the wedding ring before the ceremony."

"Avoid dressing before a mirror."

"A bride should not break anything on her wedding day, if she wishes to keep peace in her future family."

"Never read the marriage service ahead of time."

"A cat in the bride's house should be fed by her on the wedding morning to prevent rain."

"The bride should shed tears on her wedding day if she wishes to be happy; if she shows any signs of gaiety, she will shed bitter tears during her married life."

"Lucky is the bride who sees a toad, a spider, a dove, or a lamb on her way to church; if she meets a pig she should go back and start from home once more."

"A double wedding means unhappiness to one of the couples."

"A bride, in order to be happy, should step over the church threshold with her right foot."

"Dream of marriage and you will attend a funeral; dream of a funeral and you will attend a marriage."

"Never postpone a wedding."

"It is an evil omen if birds sing on the bride's house immediately before or after the wedding ceremony; but if on the way to church, many birds are seen flying together there will be many children in the family."

"If twins are to be married on the same day, they should be married in different churches."

"An American bride's most sincere wish is to tear her veil, for it is a sign of future marital bliss."

"Never put on the left shoe first on the wedding day; nothing should be put on wrong side out; but if it happens wear it as it is, do not change it."

"In olden times a bride appeared at the wedding ceremonies with bare hands, because the use of gloves was reserved for widows. Lavender gloves and dress are considered lucky for a widow to wear. It is believed that the wearing of other colors will cause sterility in a widow."

The idea that the sun shining upon a bride brings about happiness is the survival of the primitive belief that the sun had extraordinary power in the reproductive world. It is still the custom in India for the bride to face the sun as it rises on her wedding day. In Central Asia, many still believe that the bride and bridegroom should look at the sun together to attain future happiness. A Parsi bride would not think of being married before she had looked east on the rising sun.

WEDDING ANNIVERSARIES

YEAR	ANNIVERSARY
First year	Paper wedding
Second year	Cotton wedding
Third year	Leather or Straw wedding
Fifth year	Wooden wedding
Seventh year	Woolen wedding
Tenth year	Tin wedding
Twelfth year	Silk and Linen wedding
Fifteenth year	Crystal wedding
Twentieth year	China wedding
Twenty-fifth year	Silver wedding
Thirtieth year	Pearl wedding
Fortieth year	Ruby wedding
Fiftieth year	Golden wedding
Seventy-fifth year	Diamond wedding

PART TWO

STRANGE PEOPLES—STRANGE WAYS

CHAPTER I

REPENT AT LEISURE

MOTHER-IN-LAW TABOO

THE traditional dread of the mother-in-law, an integral part of modern folk-lore, has an origin which seems impossible to trace. In group marriage and in exogamy, a system of taboos seems to have been nurtured by primitive clans to prevent any sexual relations with mothers-in-law. The horror of incest among both primitives and moderns seems to have some derivation, too, from the fears of such contacts.

Among primitive tribes, ostracism prevented the groom, who belonged to an alien tribe, from becoming a member of the bride's clan; her mother, therefore, refused to recognize him as a son-in-law. That is Professor Tylor's explanation of the mother-in-law taboo. Other authorities believe that it is a survival of the marriage-by-capture era during which the bride's mother never forgave the man who carried her daughter away by force. Though forms of marriage have undergone transitions, this hatred has lingered.

The Zulu-Kaffirs require a man wishing to address his mother-in-law, to stand at a distance. He may not address her by name for such familiarity might imply an authority over her. He often communicates with her by means of a third person. If by chance they meet, they pretend not to know one another. He may never look upon her face in conformity with the Zulu proverb that "man should not look upon the breast that has nursed his wife."

Nearly all of the primitive Australians, Melanesians, Polynesians, and almost all of the Negro races of Africa, have created rules for the subjection of the mother-in-law. When a man of Celebes meets his mother-in-law, he expectorates in order to rid himself of the evil influences which may have resulted from seeing her. In the region of the Nile, a negro of the Basogas tribe will converse with his mother-in-law only when a wall separates them.

The Navajo and Apache Indians never looked upon their mothers-in-law for fear of becoming blind. A quaint method among some Indian tribes of avoiding the mother-in-law taboo was to marry the girl's mother prior to the ceremony with the real bride.

ANCIENT AND PRESENT PUNISHMENT FOR
ADULTERY

Adultery was considered a serious crime by our primitive ancestors and was often subject to capital punishment. The offender was stoned to death, or, as a milder form of chastisement, the nose or ears of the adulterer were cut off.

Arabs—The Arabs, particularly some of the Bedouins, who have retained most of their ancient customs, believed adultery to be the most serious of crimes. The beheading of the offending female was entrusted to her father or to her brother. The Koran is comparatively lenient about adultery; according to the laws of Mahomet, commission of the offence must be proved by four witnesses. Though found guilty, if the woman swears four times that her husband has been lying, she escapes punishment. If she has been accused justly, however, both parties to the crime are given a hundred lashes in the public square. When that portion of the punishment has been completed, the woman is imprisoned until she dies.

The Bible—Biblical canons declared that both man and woman are to be stoned when adultery is committed in the city. If the crime takes place in the field, however, only the man suffers this punishment, because it is presumed that in the field, no one is present to hear the cries of rapine and to offer aid.

China—The woman who commits adultery is subjected to imprisonment. If a husband forgives his wife after she has been publicly accused of adultery, he receives twenty strokes of the bamboo. If the woman is tried and convicted before a judge, she may be sold either by him or by her husband to any likely purchaser. Under no condition is a Chinese husband permitted to lend his wife for adulterous purposes, the punishment thereof being twenty or more strokes of the bamboo. Although Chinese legislation is not extremely severe about adultery, there is a rigorous law which protects the weak against the strong. The law provides that, whoever, on the strength of his power or credit, shall take away the wife or the daughter of a free man, to make her his own wife, shall be imprisoned for the usual time and later be put to death by strangulation.

The Moï tribes of Indo-China inflict severe punishments on the adulterers. When a wife is either unfaithful or is suspected of illicit connections, her husband administers a cruel beating. If a child is born of an illicit union, the deceived husband disposes of the infant by cutting its throat. The Annamites inflict the death penalty on both offenders if they are caught in the act of copulation. Sometimes the offenders suffer ninety strokes with the lash. This comparatively mild punishment can be alleviated by the payment of ninety francs to the offended husband. If the adulterer is a member of the family, the offense has no special significance.

Egypt—Although the ancient Egyptians did not approve of capital punishment for adultery, they were, nevertheless, very cruel to the offenders. According to Diodurus, the man received a flogging of a thousand lashes and the woman's nose was amputated. This custom existed among the early American Indians, in Negro-Africa, and among the Saxons of England.

It is said that in Chaldea, the punishment for an adulteress was to go about the street clad only in a loin-cloth and to be at the mercy of every passer-by. At the Council of Neapolis, Palestine, in 1120, it was decreed that the adulterer should be castrated.

Eskimos—Some of the Eskimo tribes had a strange custom called "cicisbei" which provided for a substitute in the absence of an Eskimo husband. In Italy, during the seventeenth century, a similar custom existed; the substitute was called "cavalier servante." His duties were to act as escort of the married woman whose husband was absent. These escorts were affected, effeminate men, and their mannerisms were extravagant.

The traditional use of the substitute gradually became obsolete.

The superstitious Eskimos believed that fairies would kill their wives if they were unfaithful. Both the woman and her lover were killed instantly in case of adultery.

India—In India, according to the Code of Manu, it is not considered a serious offense for the the man to be unfaithful. "Although the conduct of her husband may be blameworthy, and he may give himself up to other amours and be devoid of good qualities, a virtuous woman ought constantly to revere him as a god." But for the woman it is a serious offense. The Code of Manu provides that "if a woman, proud of her family and her importance, is unfaithful to her family, the king shall have her devoured by dogs in a public place."

Punishment for adultery in India is imposed according to the laws and customs of the different castes. Often property is confiscated for the period of a year, and a year's imprisonment is imposed. In other instances a large fine is paid; the heads of the culprits are shaved, and the urine of an ass is poured on them as a sign of humiliation. Among the Sudra, when adultery is committed with a woman of a forbidden caste, he is castrated, and is deprived of all his wealth.

"To pay any attention to a woman, to send

her flowers or perfumes, to sit with her on the same couch, are considered by wise men as proofs of an adulterous love." In case of childlessness a man can compel his wife to give herself to a brother or a relative chosen by the husband, "Anointed with liquid butter and keeping silence, let the relative charged with this office approach during the night a widow or childless woman, and engender one single son, but never a second."

Java—The Javenese punishment consists merely of public humiliation. In Borneo, the Dyaks demand only a reasonable fine from both offenders.

Kabyles of Algeria—The Kabyle tribes of Algeria do not govern themselves according to the Koran. Kissing on the mouth is a sufficient proof of unfaithfulness, and merciless treatment follows, often causing the death of the women; while the adulterer is challenged to a deadly combat. Whenever a child is born out of wedlock, both woman and child are killed. If the woman's family makes any attempt to spare her, they are stoned and a severe fine is imposed. Even when a woman is actually separated from her husband and gives birth to an adulterous child, it is killed though she may be spared by her relatives if they so desire. But, even though permitted to live, she is abused and ill-treated during the remainder of her life.

Among other tribes, although the custom may demand that the husband kill his wife, he does not always do so. Her status as wife must be repudiated, however, and in some cases the accomplice must suffer some kind of punishment to restore the honor of the offended husband. The combat which follows, however, is not of a serious nature. The marriage of the two offenders is strictly forbidden.

Husbands of the following tribes used to accept a compensation for adultery: some of the Dyaks of Borneo, Mandingoes, Kaffirs, Mongolians, Pahari and several other tribes of India, etc. Valuable gifts from the adulterers will placate Patagonian husbands. Some of the superstitious Patagonian husbands send their wives to the forests to give themselves to the first passer-by for future good fortune. (Falker, p. 126.)

Kamchadales of Siberia—The Kamchadales of Siberia have an original method of dealing with adultery. The husband of the faithless wife challenges her lover to a fight to see who really has the right, through physical strength, of ownership. The winner keeps the woman.

Persia—In Persia, adultery used to be a criminal action, and the woman was placed in a bag, thrown into the water and left to drown.

The hatred that Persians had for adulterous wives is illustrated by a passage from a book by J. J. Strauss, who relates that "on June 9, 1691, a Persian avenged the adulterous act of his wife by flaying her alive, and then, as a warning to other women, displayed her skin in the house." Atrocious punishments for straying wives were inflicted by the Persians and many other Orientals. Punishment of adulterous husbands was also severe.

Polynesia—Adultery by Polynesian men is considered as theft of personal property and is punishable by death. Yet men lend their wives to their intimate friends for indulgence in unspeakable depravities.

American Indians—The Indians were severe to adulterers though they often exchanged wives as a sign of friendship. The nose and ears of a wife committing adultery were bitten off. The death penalty to both guilty parties was practiced among the Cromances, the Yumas, and the Sioux Indians. When the adulterer was allowed to live, he was injured or robbed of all his possessions. In some cases, however, not only was the adulterer forgiven, but the offended husband sent his wife to him as a gift, often with a horse as an additional present. The women of the Omaha tribe were privileged to take revenge upon a faithless husband and his accomplice, but when the wife herself was found guilty, she was tied to a stake in the fields and was abused by the men of her tribe and abandoned.

Rome—In Rome, while the law of the Twelve Tables prevailed, the woman was the only one punished. She appeared before a family tribunal which executed the death punishment itself. This custom existed during the entire duration of the Roman Republic. Imposition of the death penalty became less frequent and was eventually changed into a sentence of exile with no right of return, and the woman was compelled to wear the courtesan's toga.

If the adulterers were discovered flagrante delicto, the husband had the right to kill his wife, and the deceived husband left the adulterer to his slaves who practiced sodomy, often killing the victim by abuse.

During the reign of Julius or Augustus Caesar and the period of the reformation of the laws, the husband who killed his unfaithful wife was guilty of murder and was accordingly punished.

The lover was spared under these laws; though, if he were a slave, a go-between, a comedian, or a freedman, his killing was allowed. If a father found his daughter with her lover, he had the exclusive right of killing them both. The Lex Julia decreed that when the offenders were not instantly killed, the man and the woman lost half of their property, the husband, to protect his honor, repudiating his wife, who was forbidden ever to marry again. Justinian later decreed that the punishment for an adulteress should be flogging, the shaving of the hair, and the entrance into a convent as a recluse. If, after two years, she was not claimed by her husband, she was condemned to stay there for life.

Scandinavia and Germany—Among the ancient Danes, adultery was punishable by death, though the penalty for murder was but a fine. Old Saxons burned the adulteress, and her lover was hanged over the ashes of the extinct fire. The Danish king, Canute, who also reigned in England in the eleventh century, ordered the banishment of the culpable man and the slitting of the nose and ears of the woman. An old provincial Swedish law decreed a similar treatment, though, instead of splitting, the nose and ears were actually cut off unless the adulteress paid a fine of forty marks.

According to Tacitus, the Germans thought adultery the worst of crimes. They compelled the husband, in order to save the honor of the family, to lead his erring wife half-naked through the streets of the villages after her head had been shaved and then whip her to death. The accomplice was hung to a tree.

The Visogoth law turned the adulteress over

to the lover's wife if he was married; but if he had no wife, his property was confiscated and turned over to the deceived husband. Later, under the Salic law, the penalties were less severe; if the adulteress was a married woman only a fine had to be paid.

During the reign of Charlemagne, punishment gradually grew less severe. In the Middle Ages the adulteress lost her dowry and was shut up in a convent. As far back as 1561, it has been recorded that whipping was sometimes inflicted and up to 1789 the penalties varied according to the rank of the person, the place, and the circumstances.

Tahiti—In Tahiti, adultery is considered a theft. Yet the lending of the wives is still practiced, and the wives who have intimate relations without their owners' consent are but slightly punished or reprimanded.

Tasmania and Australian Aborigines—Tasmanian and Australian men also look upon their wives as personal property to be used and ordered about at their leisure, and the lending and letting of the wives is commonly practiced. The Tasmanians are highly flattered if a white man wishes one of their wives. But if a wife chooses to commit adultery without authorization, she is severely punished. Among Australian tribes who are divided in castes, the women are common to all in the same caste. If one of them, however, chooses a man outside of her group, such an act is an infringement upon proprietory rights, and the adulterous woman is beaten, the guilty man being sometimes killed. In Western Australia, the men of a tribe throw spears into the body of an adulterer from another caste. In South Australia, some of the tribes forbid intimate intercourse with mothers, sisters, and first and second cousins. This is enforced religiously, and those who violate this rule suffer the death penalty.

A FEW DIVORCE CUSTOMS

The dissolution of the marriage tie has been allowed among savage and semi-civilized peoples from the earliest times. Among most primitive races, the wife had no right to divorce her husband. The husband assumed ownership of his wife, claiming proprietory rights. Under the matriarchate system, the same right was taken by the women. The Mosaic law required a formal "bill of divorcement," and, before repudiating his wife, the husband had to write this bill of divorcement, hand it to her and then order her out of the house (Deut. 24.i.). She could remarry. If she was divorced by a second husband or if he died, the first husband could not marry her again.

Abyssinia—The Abyssinians marry and divorce each other in the easiest manner imaginable. They may separate for any reason. The boys belong to the mother and the girls to the father.

Anglo-Saxons—Among the Anglo-Saxons, the husband could divorce his wife for any of the following reasons: extravagance, barrenness, a bad disposition, drunkenness or gluttony, deformity and for any other similar reason.

Berbers and Kabyles of Algeria—Among the Kabyles, the husband has the right to sell a runaway wife to a member of the tribe.

It is easy to divorce a wife; the husband has only to pronounce three times "I repudiate thee" and he is free, though he must take care of her until she is sold again. When her price is paid before witnesses, the husband no longer has any right to her. The transaction dissolves the union.

He has two ways to prevent his wife from remarrying. If, after the husband three times pronounces the formula "I repudiate thee, and I put a sum on thy head," he pays this price, he prevents her marrying again. If he wishes her to remarry, he may specify a price to anyone, but the price may be so high that she cannot marry at all and is looked upon by the tribe as a thamoukt or "prevented one."

If the formula has not been repeated three

times, the husband, with the permission of his father-in-law, may take back his wife, by paying a fine to the djemae or judge. In many places, the marriage ceremony must be repeated to regain the public respect.

The Kabyle husband may send his wife to her parents with their consent, without actually repudiating her. When the wife is sent back to her parents, without notification to them, riding on an ass led by a servant, the repudiation is a disgraceful one to the woman. Children, in this event, remain his property always; and the wife rarely finds another husband.

It will be noticed that, among the Berbers and Kabyles of Algeria, the law protects only the men; the women are not permitted divorce.

Some Arabs divorce only on the ground of adultery. Among some of the Bedouins and a large number of the Tuaregs of the Sahara, however, divorce is very prevalent. A wife delights in being repudiated both because it is an honor to have had several husbands, and to avoid any humiliation by such phrases as these: "Thou art not worth anything, thou hast neither beauty nor merit; men have disdained thee; and would have none of thee." Among some of the tribes of Madagascar, a woman may divorce herself at the slightest inclination.

China—The following were the seven reasons for divorcing a wife in China:

(1) Disobedience of a wife to her husband's parents;
(2) Having no male child;
(3) Dissolute conduct;
(4) Jealousy;
(5) Talkativeness;
(6) Thieving;
(7) Leprosy.

In Ancient China, if a woman permitted too much smoke to enter the house, she might be divorced.

The husband is not allowed to cast his wife off if her parents are not able to take care of her. She would invariably become a prostitute if thrown upon her own resources.

Indo-China—Divorce among the Moï natives of Indo-China is possible with the mutual consent of the wife and husband. The younger children are given to the mother, and the others to the father. If the reason for divorce is unfaithfulness, sterility, etc., a fine is imposed upon the culprit.

In spite of the lenient laws, divorce among the Moï natives is rare. Women are not only scarce, but the bride-price is so high that a wife usually represents all of a man's wealth.

The Moï women must be strong and healthy, for they are essentially field hands, keeping up their work during pregnancy and taking off just time necessary to give birth to their children. A second wife is welcomed with joy because it means one more hand to assist with the work. The first wife, however, retains her authority over the household. Widows have no difficulty in finding new husbands, due to the minority of women among the Moï tribes.

Egypt—If an Egyptian husband wishes to re-marry his divorced wife, a proxy is used on such occasions, for the law is that another marriage and divorce must interfere. The proxy, who may not be a Hodja (eunuch) marries her first, divorce immediately following the ceremony. Then the first husband may marry his former wife. The proxy is called a moostahhill.

Egyptian law protects the bride's fortune by a marriage contract; in the event of divorce, she may claim alimony.

In ancient Chaldea, a divorce could be obtained by the man, by writing a letter to his wife's father or by saying, "Thou are not my wife." But, if the wife should ever say, "Thou are not my husband," she was immediately drowned.

Greece—The man has the exclusive privilege

of divorce, though modern custom is gradually giving the woman more rights.

Through the centuries, women who were divorced were looked upon as disgraced, especially among the ancient Athenians. On repudiating a wife, a man was compelled to restore his wife's dowry or to pay interest on it. This is possibly the reason why Euripedes makes one of his characters exclaim: "The riches that a woman brings only serve to make her divorce more difficult."

Women rarely apply for divorces because of the difficulty of appearing in public courts. The law obliges them to live after the divorce in solitude in the gynoceum, the rear of the Greek house.

Scandinavia—In Denmark and in Norway, if a married couple has been living apart for a period of three years, the court issues them a divorce.

India—Although the Hindus by the Code of Manu are not in the habit of divorcing their wives, they may do so for several reasons. We read that "a wife given to intoxicating liquors, having bad morals, contradicting her husband, attacked by incurable disease, as leprosy, being a spendthrift, ought to be replaced. A sterile wife ought to be replaced in the eighth year; the wife whose children are dead, in the tenth; the wife who only has daughters, in the eleventh;

the wife who speaks with bitterness, for a whole year let a husband bear with the aversion of his wife; but after a year, if she continues to hate him, let him take what she possesses, only giving her enough to clothe and feed her, and let him cease to cohabit with her."

A Burmese woman may divorce her husband whenever she finds that he is incapable of providing for her. Marriage is looked upon as a lifetime union by the Brahmins. They rarely divorce their wives even if adultery is the cause. Parents and friends invent excuses to prove the lack of guilt for the scandal of adultery would be a reflection upon his entire caste. A Brahmin never divorces his wife in order to marry another woman.

In the Malay Archipelago, the woman had the privilege of divorce and of remarriage within one hundred days.

Indians of North America—Divorce due to failure to provide existed among many Indian tribes of North America. When a man left his wife without serious reason, he was not allowed to remain a member of the tribe. Among the Eskimos, separation was recognized as divorce, and one could remarry at will.

In the Aleutian Islands, the men, when tired of their wives, barter them for food or clothes.

Many Indian tribes never permitted a man to

separate from his wife if there were children; and Aztecs were never permitted to divorce.

Japan—A Japanese husband may divorce his wife for any of the seven reasons permitted in China. Divorce rarely takes place among them, however, because the Japanese wife is usually a model of womanhood. If there are children, a man will never repudiate his wife.

Among the poor classes of Japan, divorce is more frequent than among the others. But, according to statistics of a few years ago, there were only five divorces to every hundred marriages.

Rome—In ancient Rome, only the husband could send his wife away, and Plutarch says that "Romulus (one of the twin legendary founders of Rome) gave the husband power to divorce his wife in case of her poisoning his children, counterfeiting his keys, or committing adultery; for any other cause, she was to have one moiety (half) of his goods, and she was consecrated to Ceres (Goddess of grain and harvests)." Sterility was always a cause for divorce.

Many instances of divorce are cited in the works of Juvenal, the satirical poet of Rome, who mentions that at one time, a woman who had had twenty-three husbands, was married to a man who had also had twenty-three wives.

During the reign of Constantine, after he had

become a Christian, he issued a decree allowing divorce only upon a mutual basis, and prohibiting more than three divorces for each wife. At the time of Justinian, divorce became easy again, and mutual dislike was sufficient reason for separation. The Roman laws of divorce were varied until Catholicism stabilized marriage by issuing a sacrament eliminating divorce, except by special dispensation.

In the United States there were approximately one hundred and eighty thousand divorces in the year of 1925. Marriage is decreasing every year while divorces are increasing.

WIDOWS AND WIDOWHOOD IN MANY LANDS

Africa—As a sign of mourning among the Hottentots, a widow is usually obliged to cut off one joint of the little finger. This custom, though not obligatory for men, is also practiced by a widower. Similar customs of mutilation are practiced among some of the Melanesians; and the gashes on the faces and bodies of many of the Polynesian widows were made at the death of their husbands.

Formerly at the death of a king in Equatorial Africa, four wives and many of the slaves were poisoned, and if the poison given them did not produce instantaneous death, they were hung. In other parts of Africa, when a chief died, one or two of his widows had to die on the same day to bear him company to the next world, and they were buried in the same tomb with him.

In Northern Rhodesia, a sister or a near relative takes the place of the dead wife. A married relative must spend a night or two with the widower "to take the death from off his body," if his wife had no unmarried sister. The death of his wife made him taboo unless someone shared his couch for the prescribed time.

Arabs and Bedouins—A widow, according to the Koran, may not marry again until four months and ten days after her husband's death to assure her that she is not pregnant, and if she is with child, not until after her delivery. The Arabs do not approve of marrying or remarrying with widows, and attendance at ceremonies at which a widow remarries is supposed to bring bad luck to whomever attends the wedding.

Aborigines of Australia—In the Kamilaroi tribe in Australia, widowhood is impossible, for women are common wives to all men of their class. Among many tribes, however, the relatives of a deceased man cover their heads with clay, and in western Australia they use red mud as a sign of mourning.

The Levirate Law of the Hebrews—Hebrews were compelled to marry the widows of their deceased brothers as a means of perpetuating the family name. Finck in Primitive Love and Love-Stories (p. 344-45) tells us that "the levirate has prevailed among a great number of races, from the lowest to those comparatively advanced. The list includes Australians, many Indians, Aleuts, Eskimos, Fijians, Samoans, Caroline Islanders, natives of New Caledonia, New Guinea, New Britain, New Hebrides, the Malay Archipelago, wild tribes of India, Kamchadales, Ostiaks, Kirghiz, Mongolians, Arabs, Egyptians, Hebrews, natives of Madagascar, many Kaffir tribes, negroes of the Gold Coast, Senegambians, Bechuanas, and a great many other Africans."

India—In 1856, the English law permitted the widows to remarry, although widows among the higher classes seldom did. It is still a common belief in India that the departed spirit will return to cause evil if the survivor remarries. All sorts of charms are worn to appease the spirit's jealousy and to prove faithfulness.

Hindu widows were formerly burned on the funeral pyre of their husbands in the ceremony of suttee. It is said that about 1600, the Mogul Emperor Akbar forbade the burning of widows, but the practice continued until 1825 when the English prohibited it by law during the Governor-Generalship of Lord William Bentinck (1825-35). The order was favored by the great Rajah Ram Mohun Roy.

The ghost of a deceased husband was believed to hover about his widow who considered remarriage, in an attempt to separate her from her lover. To guard against such interferences, a veil was thrown about the pair at the wedding ceremony. Meeting a widow is considered an ill omen.

Among the Sudras, a widow's head is shorn once a month. She is not permitted to chew betel; she wears no elaborate ornaments; her garments must be white and she cannot take part in any public or private ceremonies.

"In 1881," says Finck, p. 660, "there were in British India alone 20,930,000 widows; 669,000 were under nineteen, and 78,976 under nine years of age. In Calcutta nearly one-half the female population, 42,824 out of 98,627, were widows. In all of India, one-fifth of the women are widows," and the treatment and humiliation they received was such that many committed suicide.

The greatest sorrow of Hindu women is to part with their hair. Ramabai Sarasvati (quoted by Finck, p. 82) writes that the widows "think it worse than death to lose their hair"; and Finck further says that " 'shaved heads' is a term of derision everywhere applied to the widows."

South and North American Indians—Among the South American tribes of Minas Uraguay, a widow is compelled to remain for a period of six months in the room from which her husband was buried. Among other tribes, a widow must live for a year beside her husband's grave without leaving it. Food is brought to her. Similar customs are practiced by some of the Africans on the Slave Coast.

Among the ancient Peruvians, a widow never remarried. It is said that when an Inca chief died, his favorite wife, servants, and officers were killed and buried with him, "that they might serve him in the other life." This custom was also practiced by the Comanche Indians, as well as by many of the California tribes.

The legends of the Greenland Eskimos mention that widows, to show their faithfulness to the deceased husbands, wore the hair loose and refrained from cleansing their bodies, some of them being so dirty that they were unrecognizable. Even to-day if a widow should anoint her hair and appear in public, she would be looked upon as an adulteress.

Japan and China—The Ainu mourners of Japan, when following the deceased on the way to the burial ground, wear their coats inside out and upside down. Widows had to let their eyebrows and eyelashes grow, wear old clothes, and never use soap in washing.

The most honorable thing for a Chinese woman to do at the death of her husband, provided

a form of suttee was not practiced, was to commit suicide in proof of devotion. Otherwise the
widow and children were sold. The Chinese law
finally prevented the sale of widows until the
end of their mourning period, at which time they
had the opportunity of becoming nuns instead
of being sold. A widow rarely married again,
but if she did, she had to suffer the penalty of
eighty blows.

Polynesians and Melanesians—In Polynesia,
and in Melanesia, natives often kill the widows.
This custom prevailed in the Fiji Islands and the
New Hebrides because of the general belief that
if a widow is killed she will be the favorite wife
in the realm of spirits. In the New Hebrides,
when a husband is away for a long time, the wife
is considered a widow, and is often strangled.

WIDOWS' VEILS AND GENERAL MODES OF MOURNING

In Southwest Italy, the Calabrian widows
wear veils and go about moaning and weeping
at night. The custom of wearing black veils for
widows is not only observed in Europe, it is a
custom which spread to many lands though the
practice of wearing veils for the mourning period
is mainly restricted to those who belong to the
Roman Catholic Church.

The veil is not the only article used to denote the mourning period. Among the Eskimos of Greenland, the widows and their relatives keep their heads covered with their fur bonnets, hiding their faces completely for a period of four days, because they believe that the spirit of the dead one is still near; the hoods are worn to deceive it and "to prevent the influence of the shade from entering their heads and killing them."

Among some of the South American tribes, widows covered their faces with their hair and stayed in their huts for many days, not daring to go out for fear of meeting their husbands' ghosts.

Among some tribes, a nose ring was the insignia of marriage, and the removal of it indicated widowhood. The same meaning was applied to a ring of cusha grass, a bracelet or even a necklace, which, when given in marriage, was removed at the death of the husband.

In the Upper Congo, among the Bangala tribes, widowers wear women's clothes, shave part of their hair, and cover their bodies with clay. The widows wear leaves or go naked, their bodies smeared with clay. This custom is observed for three months, while living in complete seclusion in the bushes, until the period of mourning is over.

At the ancient Roman funerals, men's heads

were covered and those of women remained bare; while in Greece, men let their hair grow, and the women cut theirs short.

On the Ivory Coast of Africa, the widows carry with them a piece of "fetish" wood to indicate their widowhood and to prevent anyone from approaching them, so causing their death.

Among many of the Indians of North and South America, ugly masks are worn to frighten the spirits of the dead and to prevent them from carrying off one of the survivors.

A Kabyle widow of Afghanistan is not allowed to remarry until the purchase price paid by her husband's parents has been returned. Among some tribes, the widow may return to her parents to be sold again by them. If she has a son who is old enough, he may redeem her of the purchase price, and she need not remarry. If during her widowhood, she bears a child by another man, she is stoned.

CHAPTER II

YESTERDAY—EGYPT TO ROME

ANCIENT AND MODERN MARRIAGE CUSTOMS OF EGYPT

ENES, founder of the First Dynasty of historical kings has been credited as being instrumental in instituting marriage laws in Egypt. By severity, he tried to eliminate the promiscuous habits of the Egyptians. During the Ptolemaic period, several unusual customs were upheld, among which were the compelling of a man who took a second wife to pay a large sum to his first one, and the permission granted to kings to marry their own sisters, in order to retain the wealth and the family lineage.

Two forms of marriage were observed; one with a contract and another, without such a document which listed the specific articles given as a dowry and the rights to the properties and children.

When an Egyptian of modern times wishes to get married, a woman match-maker, Khatbeh, finds him a bride whom the suitor does not see before the wedding day. The girl must provide a dowry and the parents of the bridegroom also pay a certain sum, two-thirds of which must be paid in advance; the balance being held in the event of a divorce; at which time the return of the wife's dowry is obligatory.

The betrothal ceremony takes place before two witnesses, and is led by one who is versed in Figh or Mohammedan law, usually a "fiki" schoolmaster. While the passage of the Koran is read, the bride and bridegroom kneel, holding each other's hands with the thumbs raised. Their hands are covered with a cloth during the reading of the ceremonial words. This concludes the betrothal ceremony.

After the bridegroom has thus officially met his bride, the actual marriage ceremony takes place, followed by a feast lasting several days. The festivities of the wealthy last eleven days and nights. The married pair must arrive in their home on the eve of a Friday or a Monday. The homecoming is a procession of friends, musicians, jugglers, wrestlers, and all those who contributed entertainment during the feast.

The Egyptians marry young and celibacy is practically unknown.

Their religion permits them to have as many as four wives, though they rarely take that number. However, some have concubines who incite the jealousy of the wife. In return, the wife takes advantage of her authority and makes life uncomfortable for them. A barren wife is not looked upon favorably, and a man may take a second wife for the sake of an offspring.

When a concubine gives her master a son, she is regarded by him with great respect. In the event that the wife should mistreat her, she can be divorced by the simple words repeated three times: "Thou art divorced."

Modern Egyptians still fear the influence of the evil eye. Women dress their children in ragged clothes so that they will not attract the attention of the envious. Boys are more envied than girls and are often dressed as girls and kept in the harem for protection.

Frequently, when a man of a wealthy family is married, a beautiful chandelier is hung at the door. If people gather to admire it, a jar is broken by the family with the intention of dividing their attention and breaking the spell of any envious eye.

HEBREW AND JEWISH MARRIAGE CUSTOMS

Not much can be ascertained about the customs and beliefs of the nomadic Israelites of pre-Mosaic times. We may assume, however, that they believed in demons (Jinn) and magic spells.

Evidence has arisen to prove that they practiced animal worship. Their tribal and totemic signs and their names were nearly always those of animals such as Simeon (hyena, wolf), Caleb (dog), Hamor (ass), Rahel (ewe) and Seah (wild cow), etc. Their present pork food taboo may have originated from the times when animals were deified and classified as clean or unclean according to the totems of each clan.

Polygamy and concubinage were practiced among the Hebrews of the patriarchal age. Esau, Jacob, David, and a score of others had many wives; Solomon had "seven hundred wives, princesses, and three hundred concubines."

Abraham married his half-sister; later restrictions were imposed upon marriages within a family.

At present some of the Rabbis of Morocco have been said to consecrate short-term temporary unions. A special agreement is drawn to acknowledge the child of one of these marriages, and a certain amount of money is awarded to the mother.

In early times, the girl's guardian chose the husband without her consent, the marriage taking place as soon as the môhar or purchase money was given. The smallest coin would do in this symbolic sale and was given as part of the dowry. The marriage was acknowledged when the bridegroom took the bride to his house. He could do this at any time after the formality of the môhar had taken place. According to the Talmud, a marriage was not valid, however, unless both parties mutually agreed to marry.

The Levirate Law was practiced by the Hebrews, South African tribes, Arabians, and Druses (a people of mid-Syria), and by those in the Caucasus, India, and in Madagascar. Among the Hebrews, the Levirate Law never took effect, however, unless a widow was childless. In this case, the deceased husband's brother was compelled to "raise seed unto her." According to the Talmud, a man could be compelled to marry. This accounts for the lack of celibacy among Hebrews. There is an old Hebrew proverb which says that "a man who is not married is no longer a man."

The virginity of a maiden had to be proved; "cloth in hand and the tokens of the damsel's virginity" were kept by her parents to show as evidence. If, on the contrary, she was found not to be a virgin, she was stoned.

The ceremony of the bath among Hebrews was first instituted because of the belief that a woman was unclean "and causes uncleanliness by marriage contact after menstruation, and childbirth." (Sumner's Folkways, p. 511.)

The marriage ceremony described in the New

Testament took place in a private house. For the consecration of the marriage it was not essential to have a Rabbi; an elder could perform the formalities as well. The pair stood under a canopy. The bride was veiled, and both wore crowns which were exchanged several times during the ceremony. The Rabbi or elder, standing under the canopy, chanted the ritual, holding a goblet of wine which he offered to the betrothed in pledge to each other. The bridegroom, after emptying the cup, threw it to the ground and crushed it with his heel. After the marriage contract had been read, every one in the assembly drank some wine; and friends and relatives walked round the canopy chanting the psalms and throwing rice. The procession took place after dark and was conducted with hymeneal lamps. Accompanied by music and songs, the bridegroom led the bride to his house. Along the way, every one joined the throng, and if the bridegroom was a man of wealth, the festivities lasted for days.

Little has been changed in the modern Jewish wedding ceremony. The chuppah or canopy is still used; it is usually elaborately made of velvet with gold fringe; or decorated with flowers and green foliage. It is held by four friends of the bridegroom, while the bride and bridegroom stand under it. The wine ceremony remains. The bride drinks it and then gives it to the bride-groom. A ring is placed on the forefinger of the bride's right hand by the bridegroom and while doing so he says; "Behold thou art consecrated to me by this ring according to the law of Moses and Israel." After a few more formalities, the glass is refilled and more blessings are offered, the bride and bridegroom drink once more, and the bridegroom, placing the glass on the ground, shatters it with his foot. The ceremony is ended with the singing of a Psalm.

One of the most important formalities of Jewish weddings, is the breaking of the wine-goblet. It is symbolic, a sad reminder to those present of Zion's shattered crown of glory. This custom is brought into the marriage ceremony to impress upon the minds of the marrying couple and guests, that there should not be com-plete happiness among them until Zion rises again. It is also symbolic of the duration of mar-riage, which should "last until the fragments are united."

In the Eastern countries, the ceremony differs somewhat. It is usually more ostentatious. Throughout the world, the Rabbi must always wear the talith or silk scarf during the marriage ceremony. The procession arrives before the marriage ceremony, the bride being accompanied from her home to the bridegroom's house where the ceremony takes place. After the wedding, the bride walks three times round a bowl in which there are two fish. These are the emblem of fruitfulness; and while she walks, friends and relatives repeat, "Be fruitful and multiply."

Centuries before the Christian era, the bridesmen were usually the witnesses of the physical consummation of the marriage. Later the mother-in-law was a witness to the completion of the conjugal relationship.

The same custom prevailed in India and in Rome; the guests were present at the first union of the newly wedded pair. The early Germans practiced a similar custom; the first act of concubitus had to be witnessed in order to complete the marriage ceremony; this custom continued to be practiced by them through the Middle Ages. This custom was also observed by kings, and when marriage by proxy took place a sword was placed in bed to separate the pair.

Jewish people very seldom intermarry with other races. It is said that mixed marriages are not fruitful and in the Talmud it is mentioned twice that such marriages will only produce girls.

ANCIENT MARRIAGE CUSTOMS OF GREECE AND ROME

Among the Greek peasants, we find distinct traces of the past classical period. Most of their present customs, in fact, are a survival of the traditional beliefs of ancient Hellas.

In the Greek legends, polygamy appears to have been practiced. Later we find that concubinage was tolerated by the Greek law but was not generally accepted by the public.

The father of the bride was given many presents by the suitor, but most of them were usually presented to his daughter as a dowry. Later, it became the custom for the bridegroom to give the gifts to his bride as soon as she unveiled and was seen by him for the first time.

In ancient Lesbos and Lacedaemon (Sparta), a woman was treated merely as chattel and was married off by her father, brother or paternal grandfather to whomever they chose. The father could even dispose of his daughter in his will.

Trial marriages in Greece and Rome were sometimes contracted, and, if a child was born, an actual marriage ceremony took place.

Celibacy was regarded in Sparta as a criminal offense, and those who married late were tried under that law. Marrying a woman from outside of Sparta was illegal.

If a husband was impotent, the wife might be engendered by a selected youth and the child remain in the family as the husband's heir.

Many Spartan marriage customs were cruel. The bride was often stolen or carried off. Her hair was cut and she had to wear men's clothes. Children were the property of the city, and there were rigid rules against any one contracting a union with persons diseased physically or mentally. Newly born infants were examined by elders. When healthy, they were allowed to live, otherwise they were left to die in the mountains.

In Greece, wedding ceremonies are solemnized only at the time of the full moon and preferably in winter. The Athenian women were more secluded than women in other parts of Greece and were treated as chattels. They were considered as instruments in bearing children for the State.

Before the wedding a bride dedicated her girdle, a lock of hair, and her childhood toys to a goddess. The ceremony of the bath was performed by both bride and bridegroom before marriage, and the water had to be brought from a sacred spring. After the bath, they could wear their wedding garments. On the wedding day, sesame seeds and honey were offered to the guests at the reception which took place at the bride's house. The father of the bride would offer many sacrifices to the gods of marriage. The gall of the animal sacrificed had to be removed that no bitterness might ever enter into the lives of the newly married pair.

The feast ended with a libation after which the bride's mother gave her daughter to the bridegroom. An elaborate procession formed on the way to the new home, both bride and bridegroom sitting in a chariot. The bride's mother followed, holding the nuptial torches. They were all accompanied by musicians singing the song of Hymen.

At the time of Cecrops, the legendary builder of Athens, children were named after their mothers, and Greece was called Motherland instead of Fatherland. This matriarchate custom is still observed in Fiji, among the Bechuanas, in Senegal, Congo, and Guinea.

Solon forbade a young man to marry an older woman for her wealth; and when found out, the man was compelled by "a censor" to marry a young girl.

In rural communities, a professional matchmaker must arrange for the betrothal. The ceremony of exchanging rings follows. After the formal betrothal ceremony, the bridegroom is allowed to visit the bride's family.

In some parts of Greece, when the bridegroom leaves home to get married, his mother lays a girdle in his path for him to step over. He then goes to the bride's home; the priests are present, and the two families sign the marriage contract. Sweet basil is offered to the father of the bridegroom, and a second exchange of rings is made. This is done while the father of the bride pronounces the ceremonial words three times: "Accept this betrothal of my daughter." Then the bridegroom is given a glass of wine, a ring-shaped cake, and a spoon. He drinks the wine, drops coins into the glass, and gives the spoon with half of the cake to the best man who presents them to the bride.

The best man puts the shoes on the bride's feet, while her mother spills water in front of her, saying three times, "Bride, hast thou thy shoes?" Tapers are lighted, and a third exchange of rings takes place. This concludes the betrothal ceremony.

At the marriage ceremony, crowns are exchanged three times, and bride and groom are then led three times around the altar by the best man. The crowns are removed, blessings are given, and the marriage ceremony is over. The best man is the first to kiss the bride; then the couple is welcomed by the bride's mother, who places a loaf of bread on the bride and bridegroom's heads, while the guests and relatives shower them with sweets.

When the bride leaves her home, she takes half a loaf of bread with her, leaving the other half with her parents. Later, the best man gives her a half of the cake and the spoon, given him previously by the bridegroom. The bride eats the cake, and keeps the spoon with which to eat the first food in her new home. In some parts of Greece, the bridal pair spend a few nights at the bride's home to show that there is no ill feeling between the families.

Upon arriving at the bridegroom's house, the bride is offered some honey by the bridegroom's mother who awaits them at the door. The bride drinks some of it as a sign that in her future married life, her words will be as sweet as honey; the remainder is smeared on the lintel of the door for good luck.

A mock marriage by capture is still practiced by the shepherds in the mountainous parts of Greece, and the bride pretends to resent it.

In 1926, the Pengalos government imposed a tax of three thousand drachmas (approximately thirty dollars) a year upon all single men. After forty the bachelor's tax is lessened to one thousand drachmas.

From fragmentary documents, it is possible to assume that at the dawn of the Roman Empire, 753 B.C., the Roman's fate was left entirely in the hands of the soothsayers. Romulus decreed that nothing should ever be undertaken, not even the election, without the approval of the soothsayers.

The man had absolute power over his wife and children. He had the right not only to leave his wife, but to inflict upon her the death punishment. The Romans were monogamous, making a distinction between concubines and the legal wife.

There were, in ancient Rome, three kinds of legal marriages. The usus, the coemptio in manus or imaginary sale, and the patrician form called confarreatio, the latter being the only one which was performed with a religious ceremony.

The usus form of marriage was a free union carried out by living a year without leaving the man's house for three nights in succession. This marriage was dissolved when the woman broke the rule.

The marriage by coemptio in manus or purchase, was widely practiced among the ancient Romans, and in time, became a symbol; as soon as the wife was delivered to her husband, he gave a few coins to seal the contract. Later the dowry marriage custom followed.

The marriage by confarreatio compelled the bride to be led, in a pompous procession witnessed by at least ten persons, to the bridegroom's house. A special formula was repeated, and a sacred cake, presented to them by the priest, was eaten by the bride and bridegroom. An ox-yoke, over which had been placed the skin of a sheep which had been offered in sacrifice, was used as a seat for the contracting parties.

Plebeians and patricians were forbidden to intermarry, and Valentinian punished by death those who married barbarians.

Whenever a man decided to get married it was compulsory for him to make his wish known to the girl's father first, and if accepted, the formal question "Spondesne?" was made, to which the reply "Spondee" was given. This, followed by the festival called "Sponsalia" constituted the betrothal.

The bride had to wear a specially woven wedding dress, which was fastened about her waist with a woolen girdle. Her hair was separated into six locks with the turned point of a javelin (hasta celibaris) which had pierced the body of a gladiator. Then her head was covered with a yellow net and a yellow veil, and she wore yellow shoes. After this, the bride was led to the bridegroom's house where she was lifted over the threshold. In this procession, the bride was accompanied by relatives, friends of both parties, and minstrels playing on flutes and singing the nuptial song, Hymenaeus.

In olden times, an open basket was carried by the bride in which was a distaff to signify that the bride would spin for the family. Upon entering the house of the bridegroom, the bride was presented with fire and water, a relic of ancient worship, symbolizing the two indispensable needs in life; after which followed the feast, concluded by the scattering of nuts.

The civil wars of the Roman Republic depopulated it to such a degree that Augustus (the first emperor 63 B.C. to 14 A.D.) enacted a law to encourage and reward those who married. He imposed a tax upon unmarried men between twenty and sixty and upon unmarried women between the ages of twenty and fifty.

Those who had more than three children enjoyed authority over the unmarried persons in their family.

At the time of Antonius (121-180 A.D.), a father could look for another husband for his daughter, if her first husband had been away for a period of three years.

The consent of the paterfamilias was necessary for both sons and daughters before they could marry; this rule existed even up to the time of Marcus Aurelius.

During Constantine's reign, the first Christian emperor of Rome (272-337 A.D.), children might voice their choice in the selecting of a mate.

The law of the Twelve Tables decreed that crippled children could be destroyed at birth.

CHAPTER III

IN THE NORTHERN CLIMES TO-DAY

MARRIAGE CUSTOMS OF SCOTLAND

THE ancient marriage customs of Scotland were well described by the saying, "Consent makes marriage"; no civil or religious ceremonies were necessary, the consent of the two contracting parties constituting marriage.

One of the most interesting customs of Scotland, prior to the Reformation, was the marriage by "hand-fasting" or "hand-in-fist." Rev. W. Brown, in his Statistical account of the parish of Eskdale-muir in Dunfries, says that there was an annual fair in that parish and "at that fair it was the custom for unmarried persons of both sexes to choose companions with whom they were to live till that time next year. If they were pleased with each other, then they continued for life; if not, they separated, and were free to make another choice. The fruit of their connection, if there was any, was always attached to the unfriendly person." Later a priest, whom they named Book-i-bosom, (because he kept a Bible, or register of the marriage in his bosom), confirmed the marriage.

A similar custom was recorded in "the Danish code of Valdemar II," which was in force from 1280 to 1668. It decreed that a concubine kept openly for three years should thereby become a legal wife.

The custom of sharing money was another form of marriage in Scotland—the woman kept one half and the man the other. Exchanging flowers served the same purpose, and when this form of contract took place it was as seriously adhered to as if there had been a marriage ceremony.

BIDDING WEDDINGS

"Bidding Weddings" played quite a part in the lives of peasants. Invitations were printed in the local newspapers, giving the names of bride and bridegroom, the program of entertainment, and the list of prizes to be given at the wrestling matches, races, and other games. These "Bidding Marriages" were also practiced in Wales.

SMOCK MARRIAGES

Another old custom was that of the "Smock Marriage," to legitimatize all children born out of wedlock who had to be "under the apron strings" at the marriage ceremony.

PENNY WEDDINGS

The "Penny Wedding" was so called because the marrying couple was poor and had no means to provide a dowry or entertainment. On such occasions, friends of the couple would go round with a cart called the "bridal-wain" collecting for the feast, and the money donated was given to the couple to start their new life. Guests enjoyed themselves at their own expense at a Penny Wedding.

On the Isle of Man, when a youth would not willingly marry the girl he ruined, the severe customs of the Manx people gave him no chance to escape punishment. He was given a sword, a rope, and a ring, and he had to choose between being beheaded, hung, or marrying the maiden. He usually made the obvious choice. The death of the man might have been a sweeter revenge, but the girl preferred to marry in order to remove the taint on her character. A passage in Exodus 28-16, reads: "And if a man entice a woman that is not betrothed, and lie with her, he shall surely endow her to be his wife."

MARRIAGE CUSTOMS OF IRELAND

The pagan Irish had trial marriages which were sometimes begun on the first of May or

November of each year. At the end of the time, a man could repudiate his temporary wife, and she was free to associate with another man in the same manner.

LEAP YEAR

In Rev. E. C. Brewer's "Dictionary of Phrase and Fable," we find the following article on the origin of the Ladies' Privilege in Leap Year; it reads: "It is an old saying that during leap year the ladies may propose, and, if not accepted, claim a silk gown. Fable has it that the custom was originated by St. Patrick, who was told by St. Bridget that a mutiny had broken out in her nunnery, the ladies claiming the right of 'popping the question,' which seems a particularly strange thing for nuns to do. However, St. Patrick said he would concede them the right every seventh year, when St. Bridget threw her arms round his neck, and exclaimed: 'Arrah, Patrick, jewel, I daurn't go back to the girls wid such a proposal. Make it one year in four.' St. Patrick replied, 'Bridget, acushla, squeeze me that way agin, an' I'll give ye leap year, the longest of the lot.' St. Bridget, upon this popped the question to St. Patrick himself, who, of course, could not marry; so he patched up the difficulty as best he could with a kiss and a silk gown."

An Act of the Scottish Parliament, passed in the year 1228 reads:

"Ordonit that during ye reign of her maist blessed maiestie, Margaret, ilka maiden ladee, of baith high and low estait, shall hae libertie to speak ye man she likes. Gif he refuses to tak hit to bee his wyf, he shall be mulct in the sum of ane hundridty pundes, or less, as his estait may bee, except and alwais gif he can make appeare that he is beterthit to anither woman, then he shall be free."

MARRIAGE CUSTOMS OF GERMANY

Rome's historian, Tacitus, in his Germania (55-120 A.D.) has given us information concerning the history and ways of early Germanic tribes.

The early marriage customs of the Germans were similar to those of other ancient people and marriage by purchase was practiced by them. The expression "to purchase a wife" was still in use in the Middle Ages and it is said by Grimm (1785-1862) that "it was only Christianity that abolished marriage by purchase" in Germany.

A girl could marry at the age of twelve provided she had her parents' consent, but a young man of fourteen married without consent.

Tacitus says that the laws of the ancient Germans did not permit the girls who were not virgins to marry; nor could a woman find a husband if she were not pure and chaste even though she possessed youth, beauty, and wealth.

Polygamy prevailed only among persons of noble birth. Marriages were forbidden between parents and children, brothers and sisters; and there were strict rules against incestuous relations. Due to a decreased population during the Thirty Years' War, after the Peace of Westphalia, bigamy was permitted in a few of the German states. Until the middle of the sixteenth century, marriage in Germany was constituted by mutual oral agreement, and no formalities were necessary.

In Germany and in Austria, military men were not allowed to marry unless the bride brought to the marriage a dowry large enough to keep up with the expenses of their social position. They were not allowed to rely upon the salary the man received in his official capacity.

The four principles of marriage in Germany were Kinder, Klaider, Kirche and Küche and these are the four C's of the English translation: Children, Clothes, Church and Cooking.

In the provinces, if a suitor was not wanted, a sausage indicating denial, is placed before him at his next visit. Among the old Polish nobles, a similar custom was observed; a goose was offered to the young man to inform him of the rejection of his suit.

In some parts of Germany, it is the custom for a married couple to visit the tombs of ancestors, the same tradition that the Chinese, Japanese and Koreans still observe to-day.

MORGANATIC MARRIAGE

A morganatic marriage is a union of a person of royal blood with one of inferior rank. It has been called the "left-hand marriage," because at the wedding ceremony the husband gives his left hand instead of his right to the bride. Morganatic marriages are recognized by the Church and, though the children are legitimate, the father may not confer upon them either his title, rank, or property.

BUNDLING

The custom of bundling or night visiting, observed in England and in the United States, is said to have originated during the third century of the Christian era, though it was practiced to a certain extent even among primitive people. A girl and boy would retire to bed partly dressed, and there court each other.

Sumner's "Folkways" (pp. 525-30) explains that, "having to renounce sex, as an evil, they sought to test themselves by extreme temptation. It was a test or proof of the power of moral over natural impulse. It was a widely spread custom in both the east and the west of the Roman empire to live with virgins. Distinguished persons, including one of the greatest bishops of the empire, joined in the custom. Public opinion in the church judged them lightly, although unfavorably."

"The custom was abolished in the sixth century" (Achelis, p. 58) but, "in the Middle Ages several sects who renounced marriage introduced tests of great temptation." (Lea, Inquis., II, p. 257; III, p. 109; Sacred Celibacy, p. 167). "Individuals also, believing that they were carrying on the war between 'the flesh' and 'the spirit' subjected themselves to similar tests." (Todd, Life of St. Patrick, p. 91).

Bundling was a custom practiced in Europe during the Middle Ages and it was then enacted, according to Folkways, as a "comedy of love, but not to satisfy erotic passion." Later, the custom of bundling was much in favor among the peasants of Netherlands, England, Scotland and

Wales. In Holland, the windows were built as places for courtship, and Sumner further quotes that "in 1666-1667 every house on the island of Texel had an opening under the window where the lover could enter so as to sit on the bed and spend the night making love to the daughter of the house."

"The custom was called qeesten. Parents encouraged it. A girl who had no qeester was not esteemed. Rarely did any harm occur, but if such were the case, the man was mobbed and wounded or killed. The custom was traced in North Holland down to the eighteenth century." (Wilken in Bijdragen tot T. L.-Kunde, XXXV, 205).

North American immigrants brought the custom of bundling with them, and it was welcomed by the colonists whose houses were neither warmly built nor large enough for privacy. Burnaby says in his "Travels in the Middle Settlements of North America" (1759-1760) that "it was the custom amongst the lower classes of Massachusetts that a pair who contemplated marriage spent the night together in bed partly dressed. If they did not like each other they might not marry, unless the woman became pregnant. The custom was called 'tarrying'."

"The custom of bundling had a wide range of variety. Two people sitting side by side might cover themselves with the same robe, or lie on the bed together for warmth."

"It died hard" after the Revolution, says Stiles in "Bundling", p. 75, and "in 1778, a ballad in an almanac brought the custom into popular ridicule." The custom was practiced as late as 1868 among the poor classes of Scotland.

MARRIAGE CUSTOMS OF HOLLAND

Among the Dutch peasants, courting takes place on Sunday. On that day, the suitor in quest of a wife calls at the house of the girl he has chosen. If offered a seat, he assumes that he is welcome.

When a man wants to find out whether or not he will be accepted by the girl he prefers, he calls three times at her house to ask for a match to light his pipe. The third time, the parents assume that he is contemplating marrying their daughter. If they like him, he is invited in and is given the third match. In Holland, the parents' consent is absolutely necessary, and the marriage of minors who marry without it may be annulled.

Before the wedding, the bride and bridegroom are seated on a platform under a canopy of evergreens. Each guest delivers a short speech on the coming event, while offering a gift to the future couple. Then they are all invited to join in the feast served in another room. There is a special sweatmeat called "bridal sugar" and the national spiced wine, "bride's tears", to make the function a happy one.

Before going to the Town Hall for the marriage ceremony, the door of the bride's house is painted green.

In the North of Holland, an old custom still prevails in some of the villages. Two unmarried men go about announcing the contents of the wedding menu in verse, tapping on the doors of the guests with a wand decorated with ribbons of all colours.

MARRIAGE CUSTOMS OF SCANDINAVIA

In olden times, in Sweden, a rival suitor would wait with his friends until the bride was on her way to the ceremonies to attack the bridal party and capture the bride from his foe. A battle ensued among the men of both parties, and the stronger won the bride. She was carried away if won by the rival or was married if won by the bridegroom. There were in the church at Husaby, in Gothland, many spears in which torches could be placed to light the way and protect the bride. Such spears can still be seen in the Copenhagen Museum.

The bridegroom and the bridesmaids sewed in

their garments herbs and jewels which were supposed to have a protecting influence. The bridegroom used garlic, chives, and rosemary; the
bridesmaids had jewels and bells sewed in their
dresses. The bride would fill her pocket with
bread to distribute among the poor as she met
them on the road on her way to be married;
but to eat the bread was unlucky. Coming back
from the ceremony, the newly married pair had
to visit their stock of cattle, in order to assure
themselves of a prosperous married life.

In Sweden to-day, the father usually selects
a bride for his son, but often the selection is made
by the match-makers. After the proposal has
been made to the bride's parents and has
been accepted, the suitor is allowed to see his
future wife, but he may not speak to her, for
the girl is rarely aware that the young man
present is to be her husband. In some districts,
rings are exchanged at the betrothal in the presence of a minister. Friends who are informed of
the time and place of the wedding by invitations
are asked to bring their own provisions, usually
consisting of bread and brandy, as a contribution
to the feast which lasts until the supply of food
and drink is exhausted.

A large goblet made of some precious metal is
given to the bride by the bridegroom. The goblet is filled with coins wrapped in white tissue-

paper. The goblet is a survival of an age-old custom of Scandinavia, when drinking from the same goblet was the binding ceremony of marriage.

The bride's dress is usually black ornamented with flowers and ribbons of all shades. She wears a crown; her shoes are put on by the best man. A shawl is held over her head during the marriage ceremony; when it is over, the women distribute alms in the courtyard; a superstitious custom of buying off the evil spirits. The survival of the custom of placing food under a tree as a gift to the fairies is carried out by the bride who also keeps food from every dish and gives it to the poor.

Returning home after the wedding, the mother presses a piece of sweetmeat on her daughter's lips that she may be a "sweet-tongued" wife. In some parts of Sweden there are three rings used; one at betrothal, one at marriage, and one worn when the first baby is born.

Whenever a widower remarries, he must burn the shirt given him by his first wife on the day before his second marriage.

Many of the marriage customs of Norway resemble those of Sweden. After the wedding feast, the most important formality for the bride is to "dance off her crown." This crown, usually quite high and set with imitation jewels, is worn only by a virtuous maiden. The bride is made to stand blindfolded among a circle of girls; she places her crown on the first girl she can catch and this game is kept up until every girl has worn the crown at least once. Superstitious brides sometimes wear green, but the bridesmaids always do. Guests are expected to place a coin on the wedding cake.

When a poor girl is married she may borrow a crown and a girdle, kept for that purpose from the parish. In some parts a small pine, fir, or spruce tree is planted on each side of the door of the house of the newly wedded pair and is left there until the first child is born. This custom is also observed by the Finlanders.

In Finland, after the wedding ceremony, the bride and bridegroom sit in a room prepared for the occasion. The bride holds a sieve covered with a silk shawl, and the guests, in order of their rank, file by her one by one. As they offer their wishes they drop money into the sieve. This is a contribution towards the bride's dowry. A groomsman standing near the bride shouts the name of each guest and the amount of money given.

A suitor in Lapland is interested only in the number of reindeer a bride has. But the bridegroom, in exchange must give the bride jewelry and presents of all kinds.

Intermarriage between Lapps, Swedes, Norwegians and Russians very seldom occurs and when it does, it is considered a dishonorable union. The ancient Scandinavians usually had only one legitimate wife but they always had many concubines, and brides who did not have a dowry were looked upon as concubines. These ideas are still prevalent among the peasant class.

CHAPTER IV

SOME LATIN PEOPLES

MARRIAGE CUSTOMS OF ITALY

N Venice, contrary to the custom of other lands, the bride does not wear her best dress for the wedding ceremony. She prefers to wait until the evening when, before all the guests, she displays not only her nicest gown but all the jewels she owns.

In Tuscany, no maidens are ever allowed to assist at a wedding ceremony; only married women have that privilege. The bride wears a dark dress and a white bonnet. To complete this costume, she must carry a fan, even though it is winter. During the courtship, which takes place only on feast days, the wooer must always bring colored flowers.

In Southern Italy, married women have little liberty; some are locked up when their husbands go away to keep them away from temptation. The wives consider this jealousy as a mark of deep love.

In Sicily, the mother selects her son's future bride. The morning after the wedding, the groom must hang the sheet from their nuptial couch in full view in the house, so that everyone can verify the virginity of the bride. When she is not a virgin, the husband cuts a vein in his wrist to stain the sheet and then commits suicide by cutting one of his arteries.

In the country, the courtship takes place during the harvest season. On Sunday, girls go gleaning and bring home the sheaves which are hung at their windows or placed upon the roofs. The fastest gleaner has no difficulty in finding a suitor.

In some parts of Italy, the suitor must call unexpectedly on the girl. If he finds her occupied with her daily tasks, he knows she will be a useful wife, and he immediately asks her to be his bride. If she is found idle, he returns home and his mother proceeds to look for another bride.

One of the customs of Italy is that of giving the girl a red ribbon to be worn in her hair during the period of betrothal.

Both the civil and religious ceremonies are

necessary to proper marriage. Very few judicial separations take place, and no divorce is recognized since the Roman Catholic Church forbids the dissolving of marriage.

Augustus (63 B.C.-A.D. 14) enacted a law which compelled men to marry or to pay a tax; the single women were taxed as well. The same law is again being applied by Mussolini, whose suggestion of a tax for bachelors has been approved by the Cabinet Council. Unmarried men between twenty-five and sixty-five are compelled to pay taxes. This money will be used by the State to organize and finance maternity and infant institutions. Only bachelors are taxed. Spinsters, Mussolini said, "are not always responsible for their singlehood; the failure to contract matrimony often does not depend on the desires of women."

MARRIAGE CUSTOMS OF SPAIN

The Cid's Wedding

During the visits of a Spanish suitor, if the parents or the girl decide not to accept him, the girl offers him a pumpkin or a piece of unripe quince which signifies her refusal of his courtship.

Courtship in Spain, especially in Valencia and Andalusia, cannot go on without the traditional serenade and the troubadour's improvised verses. This is the national custom. The lover, when calling at the window of his beloved, sings his amorous verses accompanied by musicians and torch-bearers. The young maiden appears and throws a flower to show her love and faithfulness.

No courtship is allowed in Murcia unless the girl's mother is present. Shaking hands or kissing is not permitted. If the parents refuse a suitor's attentions to their daughter, the lover will call upon the city's official and explain the situation to him, begging him to intercede. The alcalde or official and the suitor call upon the parents to demand first, their consent, then that of the girl, and they remain until one or the other has given a definite answer.

In Barcelona, no one except the relatives of both parties are allowed to go to the church for the marriage ceremony. The guests, in the meantime, gather at the bride or bridegroom's house, where an elaborate feast has been prepared. Men and women are not allowed to eat together. Two separate rooms are provided, and when the meal is over the bridegroom enters the room where the ladies are and throws them bon-bons. The dancing then begins; each guest who wishes to dance with the bride gives her a present, usually pieces of money, which are considered lucky for the bride.

In Valencia, about midnight, when the feasting and dancing are over, the bride and groom try to steal away. This is not easy, as the guests and relatives, amidst hilarious uproar, tease and hinder them as long as possible. In the end they escape to a bower of flowers which is placed on the roof of the house.

In Salamanca, instead of giving money directly to the bride, the guest who wishes to dance with her places the money under the crust of a piece of pie, placed on the table for that purpose.

Often, in Andalusia, no wedding ring is used. A married woman is recognized by the flowers she wears on the right side of her hair.

Near Madrid, a young man who belongs to another village must pay a ransom of sweetmeats and wine to the young men of his bride's village.

Brides are married in black silk dresses and black mantillas. They usually wear gold, pearl or emerald jewels which are given to the bride by the family of the bridegroom. The bride, who has made a very delicate and elaborately embroidered shirt makes a gift of it to the bridegroom. The wealthy and titled brides wear white dresses and mantillas.

MARRIAGE CUSTOMS OF PORTUGAL

In Portugal, a young man has very few opportunities to make his love known to the young maiden of his choice. She is always accompanied by her duenna, which makes courtship difficult. Sometimes the young man succeeds in attracting the girl's attention by pacing up and down past her grated window, and he hastily tells her of his love. If the suitor is not able in this way to communicate his love to the girl, he usually contrives a way of meeting her at church, and gives her a message of love while the duenna is occupied with her religious duties. Sometimes young people meet at a dance but very little can be said, because, the dance over, the girl is immediately led back to her watchful chaperon. A girl usually wears, on festival days, strings of coins, jewels and ornaments which represent her savings for her dowry.

MARRIAGE CUSTOMS OF MEXICO

Among the higher classes in Mexico, a courtship similar to that of the Portuguese takes place. The official announcement of the betrothal is made by the girl's driving in the carriage of her suitor through the public park. After that the suitor calls on her parents and in presence of her relatives, presents her with an engagement ring. Even though engaged to marry, the betrothed pair is never left alone. When the date for the wedding has been arranged, the bidegroom sends money to her parents to cover the wedding expenses. The invitations to the guests are double; on one side the bride's parents have their invitation, on the other side is that of the bridegroom's.

The bride wears a white wedding gown with an orange wreath. After the religious ceremony, the couple go to the photographer's in a wedding carriage which is decorated with white ribbons and drawn by white horses. The civil ceremony usually takes place the next day.

A FEW MARRIAGE CUSTOMS OF FRANCE

Among the peasants of South-East France, many old customs are still observed. If a young lady likes the man who is calling and wishes to encourage him to court her, she makes a soup, thickened with grated cheese which she offers to him. If, on the contrary, she does not approve of him, she manages to slip a handful of oats in his pocket before he leaves. If he should persist in courting the girl in spite of this reception, he is offered a red-hot poker. When accepted, however, on his subsequent visits, he is given the privilege of dancing with the girl. Among the higher classes, a young man, when accepted as a future husband, is not permitted to see his betrothed except on rare occasions arranged especially by the respective families.

In Brittany, the customs are decidedly different from those of all of the other parts of France. The betrothal and marriage ceremonies of the Breton peasants are a subtle blending of sentimentalism and romanticism, though they are always very careful in their choice of a mate.

The wedding dress of a Breton girl is trimmed with a silken girdle, which hangs down in a series of loops. Before the procession, on her way to church, her mother embraces her and cuts the loops, repeating some ceremonial words which have been handed down from generation to generation. In some parts of Brittany, the women used to wear a girdle which had been dipped in a sacred fountain to assure them of an easy delivery and a strong child.

In lower Brittany, the betrothals are arranged by the village tailor who acts as match-maker, calling first on the girl and then on her parents to express the wish of the suitor. When everything is mutually agreed upon, the tailor takes a white rod in his hand and wearing peculiar red stockings, leads the bridegroom to the future bride's home. The Breton peasants believe that if the conversation of a newly betrothed couple is interrupted, their children will be born with crossed eyes and humped-backs. In some other parts of Brittany, the desire to court is often expressed by a young man asking permission of a girl to carry her umbrella; and if he is seen walking with a girl doing so he is recognized as her suitor.

In Burgundy, the wedding feast lasts three days. One of the most important ceremonies of the festival among this wine-making people is the drinking itself. The old saying that "Franc Bourguignon ne boit jamais sans trinquer" or touch glasses, is much observed on those days. Glasses are clicked before and after drinking; and the "baiser de la trempée" or the formality of kissing the bride follows. Feasting, singing and dancing of the Farandole goes on until the third day. When the ladies have gone back home pleasantly exhausted, the men hoist a laurel tree on the paternal roof; a bottle of burgundy is poured over it and the bearers drink more wine, dance and sing round the chimney.

The French law gives parents the right to keep their sons and daughters at home until they are twenty-one, at which time the sons go into the army. In case the children do not behave according to the parents' teachings, they are sometimes severely punished. A son may not marry without his parents' consent until he is twenty-five years of age, and a daughter not until she is twenty-one.

Intermarriage between persons of noble birth and those belonging to the bourgeoisie is never favorably looked upon. Though the parents are more lenient to-day, such marriages very seldom occur.

CHAPTER V

THROUGH EASTERN EUROPE

MARRIAGE CUSTOMS OF SWITZERLAND

WITZERLAND, the picturesque, has as many varied marriage customs as it has varied natural scenery. The few million inhabitants of Switzerland are French, Italian, Austrian and German, and each nation retains some of its own traditions.

Most of the wedding ceremonies, however, are extremely simple, and the feast given at a marriage is the most important function. Nearly every one in the village is invited, each one sharing the expenses of the feast.

In Lucerne, the first of May is the day for wooers. On that day a lover shows his love for his sweetheart by planting a miniature pine-tree at her door, decorated with flowers and ribbons. If he is accepted, he is invited in by the parents, and the betrothal takes place immediately. The pine-tree is preciously kept and is seen at the window of the married couple's house until the first child is born.

The day before a wedding, young maidens gather at the bridegroom's house and make nosegays for the young men they like best; on their way home, each girl leaves one at the favorite's home. This custom precipitates a proposal which is usually made the next day at the feast.

At a Swiss wedding, there is a mistress of ceremonies called gelbe frau. She leads the bridal procession carrying handkerchiefs of various colors which are sold to the guests in return for a coin; the money is then given to the bride.

In many parts of Switzerland, when a bride and bridegroom arrive at their new home, a small tree bars the entrance. The bridegroom removes it and uses it in the making of the cradle for their first child. This custom is also observed in many parts of the Tyrol.

In some hamlets, a mock marriage often takes place, as a survival of the marriage by capture, and a ransom must be paid by the bridegroom who wishes to have his bride returned to him.

MARRIAGE CUSTOMS OF TYROL

When a Tyrolean maiden wishes to encourage a young man, it is the custom to present him with a bottle of wine. If the girl's parents object to their daughter's choice and forbid her to make the customary gift, she contrives a way of lowering the bottle from her window at night, which indicates to the suitor that he has to win her parents' consent.

The eating of a pancake by the couple signifies the betrothal.

The peasants of West Tyrol, on the wedding day hide the bride herself when the bridegroom calls for her. An old woman dressed like a doll is offered to him instead.

The Tyrolese peasants have an odd custom of distributing invitations. The bridegroom's best man sometimes acts as the messenger, but more often this is done by an especially appointed professional. Those who are invited accept by offering the messenger some food; if that is not done, a refusal to attend is signified.

In South Tyrol, if the couple is to be married a week or two after the betrothal, the bride is constantly watched by a chaperon, called the brontola or the "growling bear", so that no one will approach the young lady until she is married.

MARRIAGE CUSTOMS OF HUNGARY

Among the Magyar, courting may last several years before a man decides to get married. At that time a go-between is called upon and is asked by the suitor to propose in his stead. After rings have been exchanged by the contracting parties, the lover presents to the future bride a small bag of coins, and she sends him handkerchiefs.

The bride's trousseau in an elaborate chest is exhibited through the town. The procession attracts the attention of the people with songs and the noise of pistols.

After the marriage ceremony, the friends of the bridegroom come to the bride's house to escort the couple to their own home. Musicians head the procession and, arriving at the house, every one joins in the feast. Each guest who wishes to dance with the bride must give her a few coins and is given a kiss in return. Guests are expected to bring food for the feast.

In some parts of Hungary, women wish to be without child for at least the first year of their married life, and abortion is often practiced. But in spite of this national hatefulness for reproduction, statistics of a few years ago show that it has not lessened the population. In some parts, women are slightly in the majority; while in Croatoa-Slavonia (Czecho-Slovakia), there are more men than women.

The Hungarian dances held in inns afford the young people unusual opportunities to meet one another and express their admiration for each other. In winter people gather at each other's houses, and again this gives the young man a chance to see and speak to his chosen girl. Then when he is sure to be accepted as a husband, he has a "match-maker," usually a woman, call on the parents to announce his name and his intentions. If he is accepted both she and the suitor call on the girl's parents, carrying with them a loving cup which is the most important part of the betrothal ceremony. Jevons says that anciently, "the drinking of blood on the occasion of alliance, compact or oath," was common among the ancient Magyars.

A specially arranged speech in rhyme for such occasions is made, asking for the hand of the daughter. The suitor is silent all the time, the task being in the hands of his representative. This formality is made before the parents only; the girl soon presents herself, however, dressed in her best clothes. The match-maker hands the loving cup to the future bridegroom from which he drinks and then offers it to the future bride. This is not, however, an official betrothal. Three days elapse, in case the girl might have changed her mind in the meantime. If so, an envoyé brings the news to the bridegroom that he cannot call at her house. If she accepts, he is informed that the girl and her family are waiting to receive him. The last ceremony is an exchange of gifts and rings which constitutes the betrothal. A priest who is there on request, gives his benediction to the couple. The publication of the banns takes place during the next two Sundays if the parties are Roman Catholics. Then comes the ceremony of the "Kissing-feast." An elaborate meal is served, after which the betrothed are allowed, for the first time, to speak with each other in private, and a kiss is exchanged to seal the vows. The wedding takes place after the third publication of the banns. All the people of the village usually assist at the wedding, every one contributing some article of food or drink. Dancing and feasting continue until dawn, long after the newly married pair has retired.

In many villages of Hungary, a girl plaits her hair with colored ribbons. These are worn until after the marriage ceremony. The next day, they are removed to be replaced by a wide brimmed cap of white over black chiffon made by herself and delicately designed according to family and village traditions. This cap is the sign of a matron. The wide brim diminishes in size at the birth of each child.

MARRIAGE CUSTOMS OF AUSTRIA

In some parts of Austria, a man who wishes to marry gives the girl while dancing, a coin wrapped in white paper and tied with a colored string. The girl is not permitted to acquiesce until she has consulted her parents. The keeping of the coin signifies acceptance. If the suit is rejected, the coin is returned within three days by a male relative.

Many peasants still cling to the idea that St. Catherine's day (November 25th) is the luckiest for a wedding. Several couples are often united on that day. The best man is appointed to present the bridegroom's gifts to the bride at an early hour on the wedding day. These do not omit the traditional pair of shoes. The bride who has made a shirt by hand gives it to the best man to take to the bridegroom. This shirt is worn at the wedding and put away until the groom's death, and he is buried in it.

The wedding ceremony over, the guests play the familiar game of uncrowning the bride and an elderly married woman replaces the crown with an immaculate white matron's bonnet.

Another curious custom takes place the day after the wedding. A piece of a cake which has been concocted out of egg-shells, cow-hairs, and many such ingredients, is eaten by the newly married pair in order to assure them of the increasing number of their cattle and poultry stock.

Many of the peasants carry out traditions

which are evident relics of marriage by capture and by purchase. For example, the day after the wedding, the bride goes to church for a blessing, accompanied by her husband who is not allowed to enter; he remains outside and waits to escort her home. But, as soon as the bride appears, a great number of friends, wearing masks, bar her passage, and a mock battle ensues among them, each one trying to catch the bride and take her away from her husband. The husband is compelled either to fight and regain her by force or to pay a ransom.

MARRIAGE CUSTOMS OF BOHEMIA

In Bohemia, a meeting of both families is necessary in order to arrange the terms of the marriage.

The bridegroom is expected to give his bride the following gifts: a rosary, a prayer-book, a girdle with three keys, and a fur cap. It is also customary for the bride to give him a colored shirt sewn with threads of gold and a silver wedding ring. At the wedding breakfast, a handkerchief is given to each guest.

The bridegroom, in a fur cap, leads the procession to church, followed by the musicians; then comes the bride, carrying her prayer-book and rosary, weeping in accordance with the universal proverb. Sometimes she wears in her hair, a wreath of silver wire and black velvet, from which hang little bells and pink ribbons. Coming back from church the bride does not enter the house until her mother-in-law offers her a cup of coffee or wine. She drinks this and throws the glass over her shoulder.

During the feasting, two slices of bread are put away until the bride bakes bread for the first time. One of the slices is placed in the dough to assure the couple against poverty. When the dowry-cart arrives at the house of the bridegroom, a spindle is given to the bride and another to the husband. The one unwinding the shorter thread is supposed to be the first to die.

The day after the wedding, the bride is auctioned off in a mock sale; the husband is expected to bid the highest price to be paid in gold to get her back.

The dowry remains the property of the bride, and if the husband wishes to use it, some of his own property must be given as guarantee.

MARRIAGE CUSTOMS OF ROUMANIA

In some parts of Roumania on June 29, "maiden's market day," the display of the girl's trousseau takes place. Parents accompany their daughters, and the trousseaus are carted in chests drawn by oxen to a high mountain. Parents here arrange the marriage of their daughters; the bride and bridegroom seldom seeing each other until they meet at the altar.

In other districts of Roumania, when a girl is old enough to marry, a flower is painted on the house as notice to the wife-seekers. In some places, a girl starts her trousseau when she is very young; suitors have the privilege of viewing it until she reaches a marriageable age. If they are satisfied with its proportions, they write their names on a list, and when the girl decides to marry, she chooses whomever she pleases. Some maidens, on attaining the marriageable age, display coins and pearls in their hair, a sign that they are looking for a husband.

In Roumania, the parents bestow all their wealth on their daughters; men are, therefore, compelled to select the richest girl they can find so as to be able to start a new home of their own. A jilted suitor is usually revengeful and sometimes destroys property belonging to the bride's family.

Roumanian peasants have not discarded their distinctive costume. Men of the mountains still wear a long linen tunic, white woollen trousers, elaborate belt, and garters, with either Turkish slippers or sandals. A small, round straw hat completes the costume in summer. The lowlanders, wear a cylindrical cap of rough cloth or felt. On holidays and at weddings, a sleeveless jacket embroidered in red and gold is worn by both men and women and a sheepskin covers the whole costume in winter. The women usually wear fancy aprons; also necklaces made of beads and coins.

The marriage ceremony takes place early in the morning either at the church or at the bridegroom's house. Coins are thrown on the carpet where the bride and bridegroom are standing, while the priest places a crown on the head of each. After the ceremony, the newly married couple is showered with sweets and nuts, and the day ends in feasting and dancing. The principal amusement is the singing of folk songs accompanied by a guitar player, called "copzar." Plumspirits, their native wine and a strong brandy distilled from grain are served.

A bride never enters her new home unless she carries with her bread and salt to assure prosperity in her married life. Most of the Roumanian peasants still believe in vampires, witches, and the evil eye and wear charms and amulets of all kinds. A cross is placed at each well or spring to protect the water from corruption by devilish monsters. A small devotional altar, or ikon, is in every home.

MARRIAGE CUSTOMS OF BULGARIA

In Bulgaria, men rarely marry later than twenty-five, and most girls are married before they are eighteen years of age. Parents arrange the marriage of their children; and when a couple elopes, it is usually with the consent of the families, who look favorably upon it as a means of eliminating the marriage expenses. If a public marriage ceremony takes place it is invariably ostentatious.

Before the betrothal ceremony starts, the future bridegroom must arrange all documents pertaining to the dowry of the bride. When that is satisfactorily settled, the bride's father promises his daughter a fine trousseau. Then follows an exchange of rings and gifts, and a priest gives the couple his benediction; this constitutes the betrothal ceremony.

The feast is held in two separate rooms; one for the old people and the other for the young ones. In the first room, a cloth is spread on the floor and sitting around it are the guests who indulge in special dishes highly flavored with garlic. The bridegroom's gifts to the bride are placed in a wooden bowl and exhibited to these guests. Usually there are slippers, bracelets, earrings, a silver girdle, and a headdress of gold or silver coins. The day after the betrothal, the bride wears this jewelry, announcing her betrothal officially. A definite date for the wedding is very seldom set; six months, a year, and sometimes longer may elapse before the marriage is consecrated; yet few engagements are ever broken.

In the meantime, the bridegroom builds a house, accumulating at the same time as many cattle as he can. The bride's parents contribute to the furnishing of the house. When everything is ready, the bridegroom's parents usually announce to the bride the date of the marriage.

The day before the wedding, the girl's friends accompany the future bride to her bath, and they plait her hair. Cakes are distributed to the friends as an invitation to the wedding. Bulgarians often consult supposed witches or necromancers to learn the best way of avoiding the evil eye.

The newly married couple is showered with corn, after which the bride kisses the hand of every married woman present, and each in return gives her a fig, undoubtedly a symbolic gift for future prosperity. The peasants are very fond of dancing the chôro, their national dance; also singing, improvising their songs, accompanied by the gaïda or bag pipe or by a rudimentary fiddle called gûsla. In some districts, the girls dance in front of the bride's house and the men in front of the bridegroom's home.

The festivities over, the bride and bridegroom are left alone and are not seen for seven days. Then the bride goes to a spring in the village, and walks round it three times. She then kisses the hands of the married women who have accompanied her, and figs are again given to her.

If a married woman is found to be unfaithful, she is an object of public contempt; in older days, she was punished by death.

MARRIAGE CUSTOMS OF RUSSIA

The Russian people, serfs from 1861 and only really free since 1917, are great lovers of dancing, music, and the theatre. Their traditional legends and melodies have been retained; and their rhythmic interpretations are embodied in their universally known Russian ballet. Most of the ancient customs of betrothal and marriage are still observed among the peasants.

Women were considered of little importance; a popular Russian proverb being "there is only one soul between ten women." Previous to the period of Emancipation, a father would marry his immature son to an older woman and use her as his own concubine until his son became of marriageable age. A young wife lived with her husband's family in order to join in the work as an extra laborer.

In some parts of Russia, a bridegroom could

exact compensation if he found that his wife was not a virgin.

Formerly, a great many of the Russian marriageable peasant maidens, dressed in their best, would assemble for the "Brideshow," "Maidenmarket," or "marriage fairs." They were placed in rows with their mothers behind them for protection; while being admired and chosen by the young men. The men would then tell the matchmaker of their selections, but the mothers and daughters, were not informed until later. The match-maker would arrange for a visit; the suitor called to arrange the bargain. Fear of ill-luck prompted the parties concerned to be wary of mentioning the names of the man and maid. The agreement settled, a lighted candle was placed before a holy image while the young couple joined hands in betrothal. The day before the marriage ceremony, the bride, whose hair had been plaited in sign of maidenhood, loosened it.

On the wedding day, the father would gently strike his daughter with a new whip previously made by hand for this purpose, telling her that he was doing it for the last time, adding the customary phrase on such occasions: "Henceforth, if you are not obedient, your husband will beat you." Then he presented the whip to the bridegroom who in order to show his right as master, would then touch her with it several times on the shoulders.

The custom of crowning a bride with a garland of wormwood still exists in some parts of Russia to symbolize the bitterness of married life. A handful of hops was sprinkled on the bride's head as an omen of future fruitfulness. Another custom, was for the bride to beat her head against her husband's shoe. This was done immediately after the marriage ceremony in sign of obedience, while the bridegroom would cover her head with a fold of his garment as a sign of future protection.

Formerly, at marriage, three ceremonies of the Russian Orthodox Church took place, the Espousals, when rings were exchanged; the Matrimonial Coronation, when the bride and bridegroom were crowned with crowns of silver or garlands, and the Dissolution of the Crowns. Wine and water are given to them, a symbolic reminder of the Marriage of Cana. All formalities are made in a series of three, signifying the Trinity. After drinking, the couple walk around a movable altar three times, kiss each other three times; blessings are offered by the priest to conclude the marriage ceremony followed by dancing and feasting which lasted for several days.

Prior to the Revolution of 1917, a betrothal

took place eight days before the wedding, at which time, the bride, on her knees, gave the bridegroom a lock of hair, a sign of subservience. Then bread and salt, an almond cake, and a silver ring set with turquoise were offered to the bride by the bridegroom as a form of pledge that she would not want for anything in the future.

The betrothal ceremony and exchange of gifts took place before several witnesses. The following eight days were a period of grief for the bride, when she was expected to cry and moan because she was leaving her parents.

The day before the marriage ceremony, the bride was led to the bath, and her hair was unfastened. The ribbons which were plaited in it were distributed among the girls accompanying her. Hours were spent in bathing and arranging the hair.

When the bridegroom called for the bride, she knelt and asked her parents' forgiveness for her past offenses. When she left their house, the door remained open to signify their willingness for her return when in need of a home. The boyárin or land owner carried the holy image, leading the people to church, where a lighted candle was given to every one.

Among the peasants, it is customary to drench the parents of both husband and wife with water in summer; and to pelter them with snow in winter, in order to bring the newly married couple happiness.

Among the Russian peasants, celibacy is very rare. At eighteen, a son is informed by his parents that it is time to get married. A girl unmarried after twenty is considered disgraced.

A rich bridegroom donates a gift to the church or monastery; and the bride gives jewels to the ikon of the Holy Virgin.

A Russian bride of the Orthodox Church is not allowed to wear a veil or gloves and has no bridesmaids. Twelve men accompany the couple. A small boy carries the ikon or holy images, and tapers are held by the bride and bridegroom during the marriage ceremony. A crown is held over the head of the married pair by each one of the twelve bridesmen in turn. At the end of the ceremony, the procession passes around the altar three times.

The new law of 1927 permits only the marriage of girls who are more than eighteen years of age. Divorce may be obtained by presenting papers of identification—either the man or the woman may be divorced without the presence or consent of the other.

MARRIAGE CUSTOMS OF SIBERIA

In Kamchatka, a Peninsula northeast of Siberia, polygamy prevails. "Marriage is forbidden only between father and daughter, mother and son." A girl's inclination is often consulted before marrying, and very often the women of Kamachatka fight for the men they prefer.

The Kamchadale suitor, after he has proposed and has been accepted by both the future father-in-law and his future wife, is then permitted to embrace her if he can. The girl is enclosed in leather clothes; an old woman watches over her. The lover tries to approach the girl, but she warns her guardian by her screams; and the woman chases him away, beating and scratching his face. Sometimes a month elapses before he succeeds in touching her; but when he does, the bride accepts him by saying "Ni, Ni," in her softest and most caressing voice. The next night they sleep together.

The Koriaks of northeastern Siberia, some living on the coast-lands of the Bering Sea and others in the interior, form their communities in family groups of six or seven. There is a nominal chief, but they all live as equals. Those of the interior own large reindeer herds, which they prize very highly. A young man, in order to enlarge his stock, seeks a wife whose dowry will bring him more reindeer. The parents arrange the marriage of their daughter, and when favorably received, the suitor proposes to the girl. When accepted by her, he remains at her parents' house. He joins in the work to show what he can do for those who have accepted him.

Their marriage ceremony is a survival of marriage by capture. The couple play a game of "hide and seek" in the family's large tent, which has been divided into a series of compartments separated by reindeer skins. Parents and friends witness the chase and hinder the bridegroom by striking him. If he does not succeed in catching the bride when he has reached the last compartment; or if she is not waiting for him there, it is presumed that she has changed her mind, and the bridegroom is compelled to work two more years for her parents. If the bridegroom has overcome the bride, they both walk out of the first compartment hand in hand and are congratulated by the guests. This constitutes the marriage ceremony.

The Koryaks kill the crippled and the aged to end their ills. This is done after the willing victims have chosen their mode of death. Infanticide was practiced to a great extent, and one of a pair of twins was always sacrificed to the spirits to dispel evil influences. They burn their dead, and their religion is now Shamanism.

MARRIAGE CUSTOMS OF TARTARY

A peculiar custom exists among the Tartars on the highlands of Asia Minor. Before entering their new home, the bride and bridegroom meet one another on horseback with their respective relatives. As the bridegroom approaches the bride, he throws an apple or an orange at her, then turns back and hurries to his own tent. The men of the bridal party chase him and try to overtake his horse before he reaches his tent. Whoever gets there first is entitled to the bridegroom's house, saddle and clothes.

In the meantime, the bride continues toward her husband's tent. Upon her arrival there, each one of the male relatives of the bridegroom asks the bride to give up part of her dowry. She usually gives up a small part of it. The dowry consists of horses, sheep, oxen or butter.

In the Moslem districts of Russia there are still slave markets where a son may purchase a woman with money or merchandise at a standard price.

MARRIAGE CUSTOMS OF THE RUSSIAN
TURKESTAN

In Samarkand, central Asia, polygamy was observed as well as throughout Turkestan, and it is said that the Emir of Bokhara had as many as three hundred wives. Most men of wealth had as many as nine wives.

The Uzbegs, Tadshiks, and most of the poor

Moslem natives marry Russian and Christian girls because they may be married without bride-price or dowry. The scarcity of women compels the men to contract marriages which are entirely foreign to the ordinary customs and beliefs of the Turkestan people.

CHAPTER VI

NEAR EASTERN WAYS

OLD MARRIAGE CUSTOMS OF TURKEY

RIENTAL customs have undergone a radical change and are disappearing since establishment of the Kemalist Régime. Polygamy, seraglios and harems are customs of the past, infringements of new rulings are punishable by a fine or imprisonment. The Turkish women are not permitted to marry Persians. This custom had been in existence for a period of fifty years.

The old customs of bride-seeking and of marriage in Turkey are very interesting and most of their formalities are still practiced. When the parents have decided to marry their son, or if the son himself wishes to get married, the mother immediately proceeds to the Turkish school, accompanied by an old woman match-maker. Here they select the future bride. When the choice is made, however, the preference is always given to an older sister. Later, the mother of the girl is informed that visitors will call. The future bride's mother is very courteous during the visit; and the callers extoll the charms of the young girl. It is never permissible, however, to discuss the girl's character; that would be considered a serious breach of etiquette.

The bridegroom's mother brings red silk which is spread on the ground. The bride steps on it, kissing her future mother-in-law's hand. The bride then bites into a fruit, secured for this occasion; and the other half is brought back to the bridegroom. After speaking in endearing terms about the future bride, the mother describes her son in extravagant praise, mentioning, also, the amount of her son's dowry which is to be settled upon the bride. After a favorable arrangement has been made, the young man sends a gift to defray the wedding expenses; and eight days after the betrothal they are married.

In some parts of Turkey during the marriage ceremony, the bridegroom answers the priest's questions, and repeats them three times. The bride who is hidden in the women's apartment, is also obliged to answer in the same manner; but she can only be heard and not seen. The bride and bridegroom are not allowed to see each other until the marriage festivities are over, which sometimes last for weeks.

A more recent custom, widely observed is the ceremony of presenting the bride with sweetmeats, tapers, coins, and henna; the latter is applied on her hands and feet by her mother. These are the preliminaries before the wedding. On leaving her own home, the bride weeps and moans and pretends to resent entering the bridegroom's house. Five prayers are recited as the bridegroom enters his own house, and he must upset a jug of water as he ascends the stairs. Then the old woman match-maker knocks the bride and bridegroom's heads together, makes them look at themselves in a mirror, at the same time putting sugar in their mouths. The festivities often last a week.

Formerly, in Bosnia, the married women of the Mohammedan faith wore veils; but the girls did not. This custom permitted the man to see the girl he chose. In the old days, the Turks had a proverb to the effect that "to see their betrothed they had to go to Bosnia."

In central Asiatic Turkey, a second wife is often taken by the man, but only when the first one is old; the first wife retains her authority and her rights of managing the domestic affairs. A Bedouin woman might sell herself to a Turk, but under no consideration would she ever marry one for fear of being dishonored for the rest of her life.

MARRIAGE CUSTOMS OF ARMENIA

Ceremonies among the Armenians are a blending of heathenism, Mohammedanism, and Christian ideas, manners, and customs. Armenian parents, who give little freedom to their daughters, usually have their marriages arranged by a priest who acts as a go-between. The Armenians are superstitious and have retained the customs and beliefs of their ancestors from 800 B.C.

A certain lucky day must be chosen for the wedding, and the affianced wait for that day. It is not extraordinary to witness the marriages of sixty couples on the same day. Friday is a favorable day. The wedding formalities are started on that day while the actual marriage ceremony takes place on the following Monday. Saturday and Sunday are spent in feasting. The poor partake of the feast, for according to a superstitious belief, the feeding of the poor brings good luck to the couple. On Monday, the bride is wrapped in crimson silk, and a silver plate rests upon her head; while a huge pair of wings made of cardboard covered with feathers is fastened to her head. The ring and garments must be blessed by the priest before they can be used, in order to dispel the evil influences of the Djinns.

At the ceremony, the priest takes two wreaths of flowers, ornamented with a quantity of hanging gold threads, from the hands of the deacon, and, placing them on the heads of the married couple, changes them three times from one head to the other, repeating each time, "I unite you, and bind you to one another—live in peace."

An old custom still prevails in many districts, compelling the wife to wear a veil. She is not allowed to speak to anyone but her husband, her sisters and her brothers. When spoken to by her parents-in-law, she answers by signs; and her husband must refrain from mentioning her name before others.

The Armenian marriage ceremony of the gold threads is supposed to be one of the oldest forms of marriage, and it is said that the Priest Hipour of Chaldea united a couple in the same manner.

..MARRIAGE CUSTOMS OF SYRIA

Mohammedanism prevails in most parts of Syria. There are some Catholics and some who belong to the Orthodox Greek Church. Still others belong to the United Greeks, the United Syrians, and the Maronites. The Druses believe that they have connection with the Rosicrucians and with the Scottish freemasons. One-fifth of the Syrians are Christians; the following marriage customs are those of the Christian Syrians of the Coptic Church. They are said to be the descendants of the ancient Egyptians.

The Copts wear the same style of dress as the Moslems. The only distinction which would identify them as Copts is the cross that they have tattooed on the palm of the right hand. They are strictly monogamous; and divorce is granted only in case of adultery. Children of both sexes are usually circumcised and baptized. This custom is a preparatory initiation to connubium.

The wedding ceremony is a mingling of prayers of Eastern Christian practice.

The actual choosing of a bride is the duty of the father. Less severe rules permit a young man to call once or twice on a girl, but that is understood to mean courtship. When the father has chosen a girl for his son, he calls on the father of the future bride, accompanied by the young man. To give the young man an opportunity to see his future bride during the course of the visit, the father asks for a glass of water which is brought in by the girl. He is not allowed, thereafter, to see her until at the altar for the marriage ceremony.

In spite of this short courtship, there are rarely separations.

MARRIAGE CUSTOMS OF PERSIA

Persian kings were not only polygamous but they were allowed to marry their sisters. The custom originated from the Egyptian kings. They had three or four wives and many concubines. One of the wives, however, was chosen as the favorite and reigned as queen. The kings had the privilege of choosing whomever they pleased from the harems of others. This was a special honor to the women as well as to the man. Tertullian informs us "that the Persians married their own mothers without scruples." Yet when a girl married without her parents' consent, the act was considered disgraceful. If a girl was not a virgin when she married, she was discarded the next day. Children were often betrothed in the cradle and sometimes before they were born. The ceremony of betrothal consisted of joining the hands of the boy and girl while a priest chanted some prayers. A later ruling postponed the betrothal of the girl until twelve or thirteen years of age. Marriages in Persia to-day, however, are arranged to comply with the Koran; and a boy and girl usually marry when they are about eighteen years old.

Persian women are shrouded from head to foot in blue sheets and wear cambric veils. The women's eyes alone are visible; and they are seen only through a very small aperture covered crosswise with threads.

Marriages frequently take place among cousins who are brought up in the same household as brothers and sisters. Marriage between cousins is highly regarded among the Persians, and these consanguineous unions have not caused any apparent ill-effects upon the nation.

In other cases, young persons marry those whose parents are in their own respective trades.

Before the betrothal, a contract is drawn, arranging the dowry. At the betrothal ceremony, the bride sits upon an inverted brass bowl, beside which a saddle and a pillow are placed. During the ceremony the bride is covered with a green cloth and must remain silent. Next to her are placed a mirror, a lighted candle, the Koran, and a large tray filled with dates, tapers, dried seeds, and perfumes.

Between the betrothal and the marriage ceremony a few months elapse. A widow may marry after one month. The date for the wedding is arranged by an astrologer; and when the date is set the bride goes in state to the bath; while the bridegroom has his nails stained for the ceremony.

During the wedding ceremony, the familiar double banquet is held in the bride's house. One takes place in the women's apartment and the other one in that of the men. The bride sits on a saddle facing Mecca. Her garments are loosened, and a mirror and two lighted candles are placed in front of her. A long white sheet, a gift from the bridegroom, is swathed round her body. Sweetmeats are placed in her mouth, and two pieces of sugar are rubbed to dust over her head.

The priest is in the bridegroom's room and shouts the ceremonial words: "Do you authorize me to act as your representative?" to which question the bridegroom answers "Yes." He is again asked by the priest, "Who is the representative for the bride?" and when the questions have been properly answered, the marriage contract is read three times. Then the bride's representative is sent to obtain the bride's consent. A Persian bride must pretend to resent being married during the entire ceremony, but finally accepts and says, "I agree," which answer is brought back to the bridegroom, completing the marriage rites.

Then the bridegroom is accompanied to the women's apartments to see his bride; as he enters, she rises and he places his right hand over her head as a symbolic sign of future protection.

To induce the bride to show her face, the bridegroom gives her a ring. He sees her features reflected in the mirror, but he is not supposed to look at her again for a long time, because a husband, in Persia, must not show interest in his bride.

With candles and fireworks, friends of the bridegroom escort her to his home, where dancing and feasting follows. As the procession approaches the bridegroom's house, it stops, and some one shouts that the bride will not enter unless he leads her in.

The bridegroom then appears. As soon as they are in their home, they wash each other's large toe, after which ceremony he makes the bride a gift, begging to see her face again, but she does not speak until she has been presented with another gift.

Only a few wealthy Persians have more than one wife.

MARRIAGE CUSTOMS OF AFGHANISTAN

The customs of the Kafiristan, the land of the infidel or unbeliever in Mohammedanism in northeast Afghanistan, are a combination of Greek mythology, Buddhistic and Zoroastrian principles, and pagan ceremonies.

Boys' heads are shaved, leaving a four-inch circle behind of long hair that hangs down to their shoulders. When the girls have reached the age of puberty, they remove the filets or net-caps they had been wearing and substitute cotton caps. This denotes the beginning of the marriageable period in their lives.

Afghan women of the wealthy tribes are secluded; but they love adventure and intrigue and they always manage to have secret love affairs.

The women of the lower classes must do all the hard labor. The men spend the hours gossiping, bargaining for a strip of cloth or shopping for food. They believe that work interferes with their dignity.

The rich men of Afghanistan can afford to prevent their wives from admitting admirers to their zenanas or harems; these luxurious places are prisons to the fair occupants who long and pine for freedom.

The middle and poorer classes have severe rules for their women to be virtuous wives; the penalty for unfaithfulness is to have the nose cut off. If the adulterer is found, he is also deprived of his nose.

In some parts of Afghanistan, adultery is punishable by death if the parties are caught flagrante delicto, otherwise their lives are spared. If a husband kills the adulterer, a feud often begins. It is usually ended by the first retaliation or by a fine being paid by the husband.

T. L. Pernell, M.D., in "Among the Wild Tribes of the Afghan Frontier," relates an interesting incident which came before him in the

Bannu Hospital at which he was in charge, and which illustrates the Afghan's idea of adultery and the value of a wife.

"In a fit of jealousy, a man had cut off his wife's nose, and when he reflected in a cooler moment that he had paid a good sum for her and had only injured his own property and his domestic happiness, he was sorry for it, and brought her to us to restore as far as possible her pristine beauty. She had a low forehead, unsuitable for the usual operation (bringing down a portion of the skin from the forehead and stitching it on the raw surface where the nose had been cut off), so I said to the husband that I did not think that the result of the operation would be satisfactory; but if he would pay the price I would purchase him an artificial nose from England, which, if it did not make her as handsome as before, would at any rate conceal her deformity.

" 'How much will it cost?' asked the Afghan.

" 'About thirty rupees,' I answered. 'Well, my man, what are you thinking about? Will you have it or no?'

" 'I was thinking this, sir,' he replied. 'You say it costs thirty rupees; and I could get a new wife for eighty rupees.' "

Women who do all the field work are often exchanged for property or sold as slaves.

In some parts when a husband finds out that his wife has been unfaithful, a fine must be paid to him by the adulterer. When the adulterer has no money he is obliged to give the husband a certain number of cows.

The Afghanistan women living in the hills seldom wash, and their clothes literally rot on their backs. Many suffer from skin diseases because of this lack of cleanliness.

In other parts of Afghanistan, the suitor does not require the assistance of a match-maker; when his choice is made, he cuts off a lock of the girl's hair, throws a sheet over her head, proceeds to her father's house where he arranges the bargain; and then takes her home as his wife. When a pair runs away without paying the customary bride-price, it is considered the lowest kind of offense towards the bride's parents. A bloody battle usually follows in which the respective families, relatives, and friends join.

Polygamy exists only among the wealthy tribes. Wives are easily bought, and divorce is simple. Monogamy prevails among all the others.

The important clans, the Durani and Chilzai still believe that they are descendants from the captive tribes carried from Palestine to Meida by Nebuchadnezzar. All tribes have a common code of laws called Pukhtunwali, a combination of Hebraic, Mohammedan, and Rajput customs.

There are two distinct modes of living. The tent-dwellers, are nomads; whereas the tribes who live in houses are of a more settled nature.

PART THREE

IN THE DARK CONTINENT

SUPERSTITIONS AND FETISHES

CHAPTER I

"IN THE DARK CONTINENT"

MARRIAGE CUSTOMS OF ABYSSINIA

THE marriage customs of the Abyssinians are a curious blending of primitive paganism, Judaism, early Arabic, Mohammedanism, and Christianity. The word Abyssinia is derived from the Arabic Habesh, which means mixed. The language generally spoken is Semitic, although the old Hemetic tongue is not extinct among the Jews of Abyssinia.

Christianity was introduced during the fifth century, coming from Syria, and after many struggles, it became the established religion of the Abyssinian empire.

The Abyssinian Christian goes about bareheaded and barefoot to distinguish him from the Mohammedans who wear turbans and sandals. The women wear a crucifix about the neck on a colored ribbon. Curious silver rings and bells are worn as ornaments on their hands and feet. Men either cut their hair or braid it; the unmarried girls wear theirs short, and married women wear a colored handkerchief bound about their heads.

Some women often prick their gums blue in a form of tattooing to enhance their personal charm. They must uncover one shoulder in the presence of royalty to show their respect, and a high born subject usually covers himself up to the mouth in the company of inferiors.

Abyssinians make a sharp distinction between a civil and a religious marriage ceremony. Marriage is only contracted for a short period of time; it may be terminated at the least provocation. Children born from these temporary unions are not considered in terms of either legitimacy or illegitimacy; those of the same father and mother are greatly attached to each other, while the step-children often become life enemies.

Marriage is not considered seriously; the woman enjoys as much liberty as she did before the marriage, and her temporary pretence of faithfulness to her husband is soon forgotten. She usually gives herself freely to whomever she likes.

A sentimental courtship, with its attendant kisses, is unknown; tickling and pinching seem to be their only mode of love-making. An Abyssinian woman, incapable of love, is never jealous. Her unfriendliness towards other women is due to a fear of her husband becoming infatuated with another woman, thus depriving her of comfort. Quarrels among the women often lead the husband to a definite separation, and both the husband and the wife are free again to contract another union. The Abyssinian Arab women never ascribe any importance to their husbands' unfaithfulness; they do not show the slightest resentment at their alliances with other women.

Southern Abyssinian men do not look for virtue in girls. If a woman has had many lovers and several husbands, she is greatly admired and much more popular. A girl will unstintingly offer her body to any white man and will feel hurt if she is refused.

Another custom which prevails in the southern part of Abyssinia is the right of the women to rule over men. In the Beni Amer tribe of Mohammedan shepherds, men are absolute slaves, and the women have most of the traits usually ascribed to men. Sometimes the husband is compelled to give his wife a cow or some other gift which will go towards increasing her personal property. Then when independent and no longer interested in him, she often leaves him to join another mate of her choice. If the husband should refuse to comply with his wife's wishes, the other women of the tribe are called to assist in inflicting a severe beating or some other punishment upon the defenseless man. Women consider signs of attachment towards a man as a disgrace. They address their husbands in coarse and vulgar terms.

Among the Christian Abyssinians, parents still choose suitors for their daughters. The girl is usually consulted as a matter of form, but, whether or not she is satisfied with the choice she always accepts.

Many Abyssinians are acquiring European ideas and habits and some of them are gradually conforming to Christianity. Many of the men become monks when old, and some of the wives enter convents. Their worldly possessions are left to their children.

A FEW OF THE MANY MARRIAGE CUSTOMS OF THE ARABS

To a Westerner, traveling through Moham-medan countries, nothing appears more impos-ing than to witness the call to prayer by the muezzin from the top of the minaret tower of the mosque. Arabia is a land of mosques, market places, and cushioned coffee rooms which are an integral part of their lives. Whether in their homes or in their tents, in the deserts the Arab is generally very hospitable and considers sacred his duties as a host. The guest, too, feels bound; seldom does he enter into an act against a home in which he once partook of food.

A girl is kept ignorant of her betrothal. When she finds it out, according to custom, she must run away to the mountains. If, by chance, she likes the suitor, she only makes a pretence at escape; but, if on the contrary she dislikes him, she often runs away never to return.

At the marriage ceremony, she must pretend to escape again, crying, shrieking, and begging her parents to protect her. The bridegroom takes her to a tent which has never before been used, and only then is he allowed to exclaim joy for his satisfaction with her beauty as a public announcement. In some tribes, the face and hands of the future bride are shown to the suitor before he makes any payment to the future father-in-law.

Before the ceremony is over, a sheep is sacrificed by the bridegroom and the bride steps over the blood before entering her new home. Another custom observed by nearly all Arabs is that compelling the bridegroom to wear a green turban for several days, green being the sacred color of Mahomet, to show his friends that he has married a virgin.

Many marriage customs of the Arabs closely resemble those of the Bible. In those tribes, living on the coast of Jaffa, Yaffa, and those dwelling on the plains of Hauran, Bashan, the marriage feast lasts seven days, and the amusements are identical with those which took place during the time of the Phillistines.

The Arabs of Tunis dress the bride with seventeen garments of silk and muslin, one on top of the other. Her finger and toe nails are stained with henna, and her eyebrows are penciled across the nose in a thick, straight line. A pair of horns which have been gilded for the occasion is placed above the entrance of the bridegroom's house.

In the upper part of Egypt, the Arabian bridegroom must undergo a whipping given by the future bride's relatives to test his courage. He is expected to smile throughout this trial if he wishes to win the bride.

Marriage by capture is frequent among the Arabs, and is also popular among the Bedouins of Sinai. While a girl is on her way home with the flock, she is attacked by the bridegroom and his friends. She defends herself as best she can by throwing stones, struggling desperately, and screaming. Her resentment is natural for her chastity is valued according to the efforts she displays to avoid being caught. She is finally taken to her father's tent where the suitor announces his name to the tribe. After being dressed for the occasion, she is exhibited mounted on a camel. A feast follows, completing the marriage.

When the marriage is arranged by purchase, the Bedouins of Mount Sinai never think of asking their daughter's consent. Many husbands contracting such marriages do not allow their wives to enter their tents unless they have first been impregnated.

Among many Arab tribes the customs of marriage are simple; and the capture of the bride is a comedy of escape, the girl merely running from one tent to another until she enters that of the bridegroom. It is always requisite, however, that the bride pretends to avoid the marriage bed.

The Hassinyeh Arabs allow their women to be married only for certain days of the week; on other days, they are free to do as they please and to live as unmarried women. This custom is similar to that of the Nairs of India and is a survival of the matriarchate and polyandry customs.

In ancient Arabia, the wife was sometimes actually placed at the disposal of the guests; at other times, the offer was only symbolic. The guests were invited to press the wife in their arms, and to embrace her, but the poignard would have revenged further liberties.

The Arab husband never looks upon his wife's infidelity with jealousy. He feels she is his property either by purchase or capture, and his proprietory rights are well established. His interest in her is entirely empirical. His attitude is in accordance with the spirit of the Koran which counsels men to pay more attention to their money than to their women. Adultery is a common occurrence and separations are easy to effect.

The laws of Mahomet speak of women as inferior beings: "Men are superior to women by reason of the qualities God has given them above women, and because men employ their wealth in giving dowries to women. Women are obedient and submissive; they carefully guard during their husband's absence, that which God has ordered them to preserve intact. Thou shalt correct those whom thou fearest may be disobedient; thou shalt put them in beds apart; thou shalt beat them; but as soon as they obey again, do not seek cause for quarrel with them, God is merciful and great." (Koran, Sourate, iv, 39.)

A curious privilege enjoyed by the Arab husband is that of divorcing his wife if she persists in eating garlic.

Infanticide which was practiced freely among the ancient Arabs was prohibited in the Koran. The laws of Mahomet say that "they who from folly or ignorance kill their children shall perish. Kill not your children on account of poverty. When it shall be asked of the girl buried alive, (for only girls were killed) for what crime she is put to death . . . every soul will then acknowledge the work that she has done."

MARRIAGE CUSTOMS OF MOROCCO

The Moors of Morocco, Tunis and Algeria belong to the white race. They have intermarried, however, with the negroes of the Western Sudan, who continually come to Morocco for trading, and have also mingled with Arabs. A large mulatto community was thus created.

The natives of Morocco and the Moors of Tunis and Algeria are strict adherents to Islamism. Marriage is not taken seriously, and they are not faithful in their matrimonial duties. Divorce may be obtained at the least provocation. A man may marry as often as he pleases and many Moors marry ten to fifteen times while still very young.

In Tunis and Algeria, a strange custom still exists. The bridegroom entering his new home must walk backwards, carrying a dagger in his hands, while the bride follows touching the point with her finger tips. Another custom, also observed by the Christian Syrians of the Copt Church, is for the bride to stand with eyes closed in a public place for two hours.

Three girls are born in these countries to every boy. This accounts for the rejoicing on the occasion of a son's birth. The Moors of Morocco rationalize, therefore, that "Allah has given us more women than men, hence it is evident that polygamy is of God."

MARRIAGE CUSTOMS OF THE KABYLES OF NORTH AFRICA

The Kabyle women are considered beautiful. It is for that reason that early seductions are prevalent.

In addition to the thâmanth or purchase money, a bridegroom presents food to the father of the future bride, a custom which gives rise to the saying among them, when a girl is married, that the father "has eaten his daughter."

A married Kabyle woman is virtually a slave. Throughout the rest of her life, she is forced to work. When she gives birth to a son, the news is heralded throughout the village, but the birth of a girl brings nothing but ridicule and abuse. Formerly, female children were left to die.

A wife owns only her clothes. The husband may chastise her with any weapon, for he is the master and has the right to return her to her parents. A woman of years or a sterile woman is not always punished, though she is often abandoned and becomes a public prostitute in the market places. Among some of the Touareg tribes, a woman hides her mouth with her garment as a sign of respect for the man with whom she speaks.

MARRIAGE CUSTOMS OF THE ZULU-KAFFIRS OF
AFRICA

There is no courtship among the Zulu-Kaffirs of Africa. The parents have the right to dispose of the female children at will. At the Ukulobol-iska or "Matrimonial-market," girls may be purchased, the lowest price being an ox, though the average is about ten heads of cattle. When a girl's charms are exceptional, the price may range from fifty to eighty heads of cattle. The price they bring in the market is the source of much rivalry among the women.

If a man contracts to buy an ugly or older woman and is unable to deliver the full purchase price, he is given time to do so. A man who has no property is doomed to bachelorhood. The daughter who refuses to accept her parents' chosen suitor, often runs away and joins another tribe.

As soon as a child is born, a hair from a sacred cow is tied about his neck to vouchsafe happiness. A cow becomes sacred when given by a father to his daughter at her marriage. From that time on the ubulunge, the "doer of good" or any of its offspring, must not be killed.

If a wife bears many children and retains her health, her father often asks for more cattle from her husband. If she is weak and unfruitful, her husband may return her to her parents and re-claim his cows. In the event of her having a sister of marriageable age, he may exchange his wife for the sister.

Among some of the Zulu tribes, a woman who wishes to marry goes about from kraal to kraal, seeking a husband; if she is accepted, a goat is killed and a feast follows. If not wanted, she is given a burning brand to indicate a lack of fire in that kraal for her. She continues her search until she finds a man willing to marry her. Some-times her father or brother accompanies her on the quest.

Formalities over, the maiden enters the pros-pective groom's hut where they are left alone for a short time, the families of both remaining out-side. She may still signify her rejection of the suitor by leaving his hut alone. The father must then return the cattle to the disappointed lover.

The Zulu-Kaffirs are polygamous. They judge one another's wealth by the number of wives. The dignity of a household increases each time a new wife is added to it. The husband, accord-ing to traditional law, must devote three con-secutive days and nights to each wife. There is no jealousy among the wives, and often because of heavy work, a wife may beg her husband to add another wife to the household. A wife is often ashamed to be married to a man who can not afford others.

Marriages between first cousins are not permitted. Inhabitants of the same village are prohibited against marrying, since they are supposed to be related to one another. Hatred against incestuous unions is prevalent. Whenever incest is committed, the girl is usually sent out of the tribe, and the man is flogged. On the other hand, mothers and sons may commit incest without social ostracism. A husband often offers his wife or wives to visitors as a mark of hospitality.

The Zulus on the border of Pondoland believe that sterility or the giving of birth to cripples is due to consanguineous marriages. They also believe that a child born out of wedlock or of an incestuous union will be deformed as a penalty for the parents' crime.

Sumner says in his Folkways (p. 269) that "formerly a Kaffir would work in the diamond mine for three marks a day until he got enough to buy cattle, a wife, a European suit, a kettle, and a rifle. Then he went home and set up an establishment. He would return to earn more so that he could buy more wives, who would support him to his life's end." The Kaffir sits and smokes while his wives toil during the greater part of the day. He sometimes assists them at tasks which require very little physical exertion.

Among the Bushmen, one of the most uncivilized tribes of Africa, girls are married before they have reached puberty. At the first signs of impotency in a woman, the men take another wife. Bushmen, though, are occasionally subject to beatings by their wives.

The first prerequisite to marriage for a youth of the Bechuana and Kaffir tribes of the south of Zambesi, is the killing of a rhinoceros.

Among the Madi tribes in central Africa, a man responsible for the seduction of a maid and consequent bastardy is compelled to marry the girl and pay her parents the price of a bride.

Among many African tribes, a girl may not be married until a group of matrons verify her virginity; if unchaste, she is sent back to her parents and any money paid is returned to the bridegroom. Many African natives will not take to wife a woman whose generative organs have not been sewn together since puberty as a protection to chastity.

MARRIAGE CUSTOMS OF MADAGASCAR

The Malagasy religious ceremonies are a mixture of animistic beliefs and rites. Polygamy is practiced exclusively. Among the more savage tribes, betrothals take place at birth. The wedding feast is the only marriage ceremony.

Women are looked upon as the equals of the men; their advice is usually considered of value.

Neither the Betsimisaraka or Sakalava tribes permit marriage between cousins for such a union would be unlucky for the relatives of both families. They also forbid a brother to speak to or to sit beside his sister; considering this law a preventative of incestuous relations. The Antamabahuaka is more savage and cruel than any other native of Madagascar. This tribe sometimes tolerates incest.

If a man remains away from home for a period of time specified by custom, his wife is permitted to have intercourse with another man.

The Malagasy people have no formal religion yet they seem to believe in a supreme being whom they call Andriàmanitra. "The Fragrant One," and Zànahàry, "The Creator." These two names are known and recognized by all the natives of Madagascar. They are superstitious and believe in charms to dispel evil influences. Since the Island of Madagascar became a French colony in 1896, however, the spread of Christianity has eliminated most of the barbarous practices.

CHAPTER II

FROM INDIA'S CORAL STRANDS TO THE CHERRY BLOSSOMS IN JAPAN

THE DIFFERENT FORMS OF MARRIAGE IN INDIA

THOUGH the Europeans have dwelt in India for more than three centuries, their efforts to impose upon the natives the rules of western civilization have failed to change the polytheistic and idolatrous practices of the Hindu.

The ancient marriage ceremonies of Indian castes are long and complicated. Eight forms of marriage are known to have been in practice. The first three, in use among the rich, were similar, and were known as brahmin, daiva, or prajapatye. One of these forms was used when a girl's father offered her to the family of a man as a bride with a dowry of jewels and clothes. If cows were given to the girl's parents, the marriage was called arsha.

These four forms were those of the Brahmins; the highest of the four castes of India; but among other castes whenever money was given to the parents of the girl the ceremony was known as an "asura" marriage. An elopement or secret marriage was called "gandharva," but was frowned upon because it pre-supposed love and passion, both of which had no place in the Hindu code of ethics. If a girl was forced into marriage, the union was called "rakshaha." The last form, a "paisacha" marriage, although never legally recognized, was that consummated by trickery.

A curious ceremony is that of the marriage to a tree, usually resorted to as a means of evading various customs and laws of the Brahmins of Southern India. The eldest son, for example, must be the first to wed. If his younger brother desires to marry first, he evades the law by persuading his unmarried older brother to become the husband of the spirit dwelling in the tree. The usual wedding ceremony is used.

Third marriages, considered unlucky as well as illegal, are evaded by the widower who wishes to marry for the third time, by first wedding the acacia tree, "babul"; he can then marry a woman as fourth wife without incurring the displeasure of either the law or the gods.

A family without children may secure a son by wedding a high-caste Brahmin to a tulasi plant, a member of the mint family, and the man lives with them thereafter, bearing their name.

Hindus intermarry among themselves, avoiding unions with other nations. First cousins, uncles, and nieces intermarry.

Formerly, a man could have several wives and as many concubines as he desired for purposes of procreation. The children of concubines are considered illegitimate. At present, a man takes a second wife only when the first wife is barren or has had only daughters, but he must always have the consent of his first wife who retains all authority in the household, even though another woman is added to it.

In Assam, North East India, the freedom of women is especially conspicuous among the Khasis who enlist the primitive matriarchate system. A man is often compelled to live at his mother-in-law's home until one or more children are born. Some may visit their wives only after sunset. The husbands of the Khasis tribes are always subordinate to the women.

In Burma, East British India, cohabitation constitutes marriage. The lack of ceremony does not lessen the seriousness of their union. The women do not assume the husband's name. A woman has a right to a half portion of the property and the authority to rule over her children. If she wishes to leave her husband, she gives him approximately thirty-two rupees. This, with the consent of both parties legalizes a divorce in Burma. Children remain with the mother.

The strangest form of marriage is the one called "wedding-funeral" still observed in some parts of India. If anyone of importance dies, the body is not buried until a wedding takes place. A platform is erected at the dead man's house, and the people of the village gather there to witness both ceremonies.

The Nair or Naimar women of Malabar are polyandrous. They marry as many as twelve husbands and cohabit with each in turn for ten days or more at a time. No quarrels take place and all seem to be satisfied. A man is at liberty to marry as often as he chooses but children naturally in this complex relationship, know only their mothers. Polyandry is practiced in Kashmir, in the Himalayas, among the Todas and Koorgs and also in Ceylon, New Zealand, Australian Aborigines and in the Aleutian Archipelago.

MARRIAGE CUSTOMS OF CHINA

Most of the marriage customs of the Chinese have undergone little change since the time of Confucius (500-551-478 B.C.), though prior to that time, ancient Cathay adhered to traditions of the Dragon worshippers.

Historical records mention the first marriage ceremony instituted by the Emperor Fu-hi 2852-2738 B.C.; which gave the husband rights he had not formerly had under the matriarchate system. The Chinese practiced marriage by purchase.

Among some of the Chinese tribes, the husband lived at the bride's home until she had her first child. No consanguineous unions were allowed, and persons of the same surname were forbidden to marry. Actors, boat-men, policemen, etc., were permitted to marry in their own classes.

The law formerly permitted the marriage of eight-year old girls, but now the legal age is sixteen. Virgins at the age of twenty-two are not considered to have fulfilled their mission in life. "In 189 A.D., a law subjected unmarried women between the ages of fifteen and thirty to a poll of five times the ordinary amount." (Tyau, p. 66.)

Ancestral worship being an integral part of the nation's religious customs, men who die without leaving a son to perform the various rites and sacrifices over his tomb, are considered unfortunate. The belief resembles very strongly that of the Hebrews.

The dwarfing of the feet of women has been the custom for many centuries, but recently, in parts of China, a tax of three dollars has been imposed upon every woman whose feet are not unbound before the age of thirty. This custom has many legendary origins; it is believed to have been instituted to prevent the women from running away.

Another legend places the origin of the custom at a time when a girl of royal rank was born with deformed feet. The practice of binding the feet was adopted by royal decree throughout the land so that the princess might not be considered unusual.

A mother usually selects the wife for her son. There is sometimes an exchange of letters between the respective families. These letters must be written on red paper, symbolic of joy. A section in the penal code specifies that the "betrothal presents and marriage articles once exchanged, the parents are considered irrevocably obliged to have their children marry." Most marriages are arranged with the assistance of professional match-makers, and the suitor may not see his bride until the wedding night.

In the event that one or both die before the marriage ceremonies, the rites take place just the same. The betrothed pair must be united. If the man dies, the fiancée is regarded as a widow; and she either commits suicide or spends the rest of her life in mourning.

A betrothed girl is not permitted to leave the house for fear of seeing her future husband.

After the ceremony, the bride is led to her

bedroom to dress as a married woman, and the hair is plucked from her forehead.

A Chinese woman formerly became the slave of her husband and his family. In some parts of China to-day the husband and wife are never seen together in public. The only time the wife enjoys her husband's company is in the privacy of their apartment; and even then, she is not permitted to show her affection and must maintain perfect decorum.

When the wife is childless, either the husband or his mother chooses another woman to bear him children. A wife who has given birth to a child is not spoken to by her husband until a month later, nor are any visitors allowed to enter the house.

A Chinese household is composed of a large number of persons, including as many concubines as the husband can afford to keep. All the children are raised as one family.

Among the poorer classes, a married woman waits at the table when her husband and male children are eating. She may not speak, and after she has lighted their pipes, she eats what remains. Kissing is forbidden; rubbing noses, biting, or smelling each other is a sign of affection.

The marriage customs of Mongolia and Tibet

are much like those of China. In some parts of Tibet, when a girl remains three days in her suitor's home, she is considered married. There is no ceremony other than the prayers of the lamas for the couple's happiness. If a husband kills his wife and cannot pay the customary fine, he is imprisoned as a murderer and suffers severe punishment.

Polyandry is practiced to a great extent. A woman may marry a whole family of brothers; they are all recognized as legal husbands. Children look upon the oldest man among the husbands as their father; all the others are called uncles. A woman is also permitted to have a lover.

Among the Moï tribes of Indo-China, a girl often bears a child before her marriage to prove her fertility, killing it if no man claims it as his own. Incestuous intercourse is practiced without disapproval, and men are often the fathers of their own daughters' children.

In Cambodia, Indo-China, cohabitation before marriage is tolerated. If a woman becomes pregnant, however, she is arrested and is forced to reveal the name of the man. The lover named is compelled to marry her and to pay a fine, "The Price of Shame," to her parents. The girl is beaten. But care is taken to prevent a miscarriage: a depression is dug in the earth, and she is made to lie, during the beating, in such a position as to protect the enlarged abdomen.

A strange custom, prevalent here, was also found among ancient Germans, and Anglo-Saxons. This is the witnessing of the first intercourse by the bridal pair.

The Champa of Siam permitted the women to choose their husbands, undoubtedly a survival of the matriarchate system. In northern Siam, gifts of fermented fish mixed with pounded rice, and betel nuts, chewing bark, and silks are exchanged as a sign of betrothal. At the wedding feast, the girls squirt a bad smelling liquid over the young men; they may only escape by paying a heavy ransom.

A woman can only receive part of her dowry after the birth of her first child. Women are generally well treated. Polygamy exists among the richer tribes, but the first wife always retains her rights when concubines are added to the household.

Tyau, in his book, "China Awakened," described on Page 71, the modern marriage ceremonies as follows:

"The marriage ceremony is becoming less elaborated: in fact, new ritual is simplicity itself when compared with the old cumbersome procedure; which sometimes required days to complete! If the parties are Christians, the ceremony may be held in a place of worship, which may be a church, or Y.M.C.A. hall. Otherwise the rites may be celebrated at a private house or public institution. The following is typical of the ceremony observed at a modern Chinese marriage. It was prescribed for a fashionable wedding between the daughter of a cabinet minister and the son of an ex-governor, which took place in Peking at noon on New Year's Day, 1918, at the former's residence:—

1: Music.

2: Guests enter.

3: The go-betweens enter.

4: The heads of the two families enter.

5: The bride and bridegroom bow twice to each other.

6: The bride and bridegroom exchange tokens and testimonials.

7: The bride and bridegroom face northward and then the go-betweens. Two bows.

8: The bride and bridegroom thank the male guests. One bow.

9: The bride and bridegroom thank the female guests. One bow.

10: The bride and bridegroom face northward and honor the family ancestors. They burn incense, offer wines, kneel, make three prostrations, and then rise.

11: The bride and bridegroom tender respects to their parents. Three bows.

12: The family elders render their respects. Three bows.

13: Other relatives render their respects. One bow.

14: The ceremony is concluded.

MARRIAGE CUSTOMS OF KOREA

The peninsula of Korea in the Far East has been designated as "The Hermit Kingdom," "The Land of the Morning Calm," and "Chosen." The latter name, used for five centuries, was substituted for "Korea" when this land was annexed by Japan on August 22, 1910.

During the Kija dynasty, a thousand years ago, Chinese law was introduced, but the Korean natives have not noticeably changed their customs. Their physical features are distinctly different from those of their Chinese and Japanese neighbors.

In ancient Korea, men and women were at liberty to choose their own mates. The mandarins, or civil officials, were permitted to have many wives and concubines in their "yamens" as late as the middle of the nineteenth century.

In many parts of Korea, girls at the age of eight literally become slaves and live in strict seclusion. Girls and boys are kept in separate quarters; the girl is brought up to believe that she would be disgraced if a man were to see her face. The girls hope for early marriages for they then become free. They make model wives, are very proud of their husbands, are free to voice their opinions in society. The women are exceptionally fertile, but, unfortunately, throughout Korea practically every child is born with a scrofulous taint.

To a Korean youth, marriage is emancipation; unmarried, he is looked upon as a child. Whatever he says or does is taken lightly; he is called a yatow, a name also given to Chinese girls who are unmarriageable. A married man, whatever his age may be, has the right to ill-treat an older celibate who dares not complain for fear of worse abuse.

Unmarried persons of both sexes are recognized by the manner of dressing the hair. A young man wears his in a queue down his back and goes bareheaded. When he is married, the queue is wound on the top of his head, and he has the privilege of either wearing the large Korean hat or of carrying an umbrella. He takes part in all activities, though he may be very young. Unmarried men who arrange their hair in married-men-style, in order to avoid ridicule, are severely punished if discovered.

The night before the wedding, a girl arranges the hair of the bride; the bridegroom has a boy arrange his. The bride must undergo a curious transformation in her preparation for the wedding. Her face is completely covered with white powder; a spot of red paint decorates her forehead; and, her eyelids are gummed together to seal her eyes. A loose, sleeveless garment completes her bridal make-up.

After the ceremony, the bride's veil is removed; her eyes are unsealed, and they see each other for the first time. Among the higher classes, the bride refrains from answering any questions or compliments. Her husband often teases her, trying to make her speak, but she must remain silent, a rule of Korean etiquette.

Koreans are permitted only one wife. Women are regarded as inferiors, and a man of the upper class must never display any affection toward his wife. For that reason, after having been in the company of his bride for a few days, he is compelled to absent himself for a long time in order to show that he has not become attached to her.

Before marriage, a girl has no name. She is called "it" or "that." As soon as she is married, she becomes a human being, though, when she has a son, she is usually referred to as "the mother of So-and-so's son."

Married women of the better classes never go out unless they are heavily veiled. Widows may marry again; but it is not considered proper because of the respect due to their dead husbands. Koreans practice ancestor-worship. Their belief in malignant demons causes them to spend nearly everything they earn in paying sorcerers to act as intermediaries for the propitiation of evil spirits. Confucianism, however, is generally practiced.

MARRIAGE CUSTOMS OF JAPAN

The sentimental inhabitants of the islands of Japan are still imbued with symbolistic ideals and superstitious fears. Their marriage customs are delightfully subtle, and though they have been trained not to display their emotions, their romantic hearts often lead them to love-matches and elopements. A great many dual suicides take place here, for when a man and woman cannot be married because of the families' objection, they enter into a death pact. The western freedom is naturally envied by them.

Throughout Japan there are many interesting customs of courtship. When a man has chosen a young lady, he announces his passion by placing a shrub at her door. If the shrub is neglected he knows that he has not been accepted; but if it is taken care of, he is welcomed as a suitor. If the young maiden wishes to express her admiration and love, she blackens her teeth; and after marriage plucks her eyebrows.

Another old custom, no longer in use, was that of having the suitors inscribe their names on a small board which was hid between the mats of the ante-chamber of the girl's house. The board was left in its place until the girl decided to get married; with the aid of her parents, she then selected one of them.

There are very few unmarried persons in Japan. When there are only girls in a family, a husband is often chosen for the eldest daughter. He remains with her people assuming her family's name. The men who give up their own names for that of a girl's are called muke-yoshis, adopted son-husbands. Rich girls avoid a mother-in-law by bringing their husbands into their own families in the same manner. There is a Japanese proverb which says that "if you have so much as a pound of bad rice, don't become a muke-yoshi." This emphasizes the disapproval of such unions.

Japanese girls marry when they are about sixteen years of age and the men at twenty.

A Japanese bride, contrary to oriental customs, wears white instead of red in the marriage procession. In order to dispel the evil spirits, two men lead the march, waving a red cloth.

The bride, as she enters the bridegroom's house, faces two immense candles tied together by their own wicks. One of the relatives of the bridegroom lights them. This symbolizes the union of their souls and bodies. After the candles have burnt for a while, they are blown out to signify a common death as well as a common life. A domestic god, images of the family's patron saints and many symbolic plants, are displayed on an altar. Two girls are dressed as butterflies as the emblem of Japanese conjugal fidelity. These girls offer the guests a warm, fermented rice-liquor called "saki"; and the actual tying of the marriage knot in the Japanese ceremony is the drinking of this wine. Nine cups of wine must be drunk by both the bride and bridegroom, the bride handing them over to her husband in a series of three.

Many religions are adhered to by the Japanese. Shintoism has 14 sects; Buddhism has 12 sects, comprised of 56 denominations. In 1915, there were 49,746 Shinto shrines, and 71,653 minor shrines; also 14,619 priests. The Buddhist temples numbered many thousands, while there were 51,584 high priests and priestesses and 8,337 disciples. Aside from these there were 2,381 licensed preachers, 1,411 churches and mission stations of the Protestant, Roman Catholic and Greek Churches. The Roman Catholics have had an episcopate of one archbishop and three bishops in Japan since the year 1891. There is no State religion and no State support for religion; but the chief form of worship is Shintoism.

Marriage is always an expensive affair, and sometimes the bridegroom is in debt for many years after. When an elopement occurs, the parents of both families usually forgive the returned pair.

A Japanese has only one wife, but, as in China, he may have as many concubines as he can afford. The Japanese believe the Bible immoral and non-religious. They believe that their chief duty is towards the parents, not the wife; and if ever a Japanese neglects his parents he is looked upon as an outcast.

In ancient Japan, parents sold their daughters to the government at the age of fourteen. The girls were educated and lived as courtesans for a period of years. When discharged, they were allowed a reasonable sum of money for a dowry. These girls were not considered dishonorable, for after leaving these institutions, they found good husbands who thought nothing of the past occupation of their wives. Geisha girls are often trained in the art of singing and dancing at the age of seven. They remain with their employers until they marry. Geisha girls, however, are educated entertainers and are not classified as prostitutes.

A tree is planted near the house whenever a male child is born. This tree is cut at the time of his marriage and the wood is used to make chests which are kept in his family and used for the clothes of his bride and himself.

The Ainus are a people inhabiting the most northern part of the islands of Japan, and are the possible aborigines of the Japanese. All female children are tattooed so weirdly about the lips that they appear to be wearing a mustache. Formerly, the Ainus tattooed their foreheads, hands and fingers in symbolic designs denoting their rank and age; the women had rings and bracelets tattooed on their fingers and wrists at the time of marriage. This was the symbol of their married state.

The peasant women of Japan are said to be the happiest wives, because they are obliged to work side by side with their husbands and are therefore considered equal.

CHAPTER III

LITTLE KNOWN PEOPLES OF THE SOUTH SEAS

MARRIAGE CUSTOMS OF THE AUSTRALIAN ABORIGINES

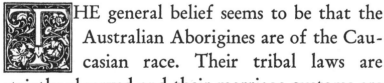

THE general belief seems to be that the Australian Aborigines are of the Caucasian race. Their tribal laws are strictly observed and their marriage customs are carried out according to each totemic or tribal organization; severe punishment is inflicted upon both men and women who marry outside of their tribes.

Nearly all of the Australian Aborigines have a ceremonial initiation which takes place at the age of puberty of both girls and boys. The boys must have their bodies smeared with red ochre to be initiated. They, as well as the girls, must also be tattooed. The designs of tattooing differ in every tribe, so that identification is easy. There is also a design incised when the marriageable age has been reached. Circumcision often takes place at the ceremony and a few teeth in the upper jaw are knocked out for the women think white teeth ugly. Their skin, which is generally oiled with fish-oils, emits a very disagreeable odor.

For the final initiation ceremony of both boys and girls who have reached the age of puberty, the bullroarer or sacred "tundun" is swung, making a booming and humming noise. This instrument, which has never been seen by them before the initiation, is supposed to have hidden power. Among some tribes it was worshipped and looked upon with reverential awe. It is a strip of wood with a hole at one end to which a string is attached.

When a woman has no children, her husband burns her girdle while she is asleep to reproach her for her barrenness. On the other hand, if she has children she discards it of her own accord after the first or second child.

Many parents practice the custom of betrothing their children before they are born or at an early age. The desire for marriage by capture still prevails, however, among many Australian girls.

Girls are married when ten or twelve years of age, very few are virgins when they reach the age of puberty, and most of them are not only wives, but mothers, at the age of fourteen. In many tribes, girls of eight years are often the wives of men as old as fifty. Among the Birria tribe, infanticide is practiced until they are almost thirty years old, and then they start to raise a family.

In North Queensland, it is said that "if a woman is good looking all the men want her." The most influential chiefs are compelled to fight for the right to possess a woman. The majority of the young men, therefore, wait a long time before they marry as they lack the courage to fight the requisite duel. Even if they win, they are kept in constant fear of being punished by the influential losers. In West Victoria, when a young chief desires a woman who belongs to another chief who already has more than two wives, he challenges him to a combat.

Among the Australian Aborigines, some tribes intermarry according to the communal custom. Marriages by capture still exist, but more often the bargain is made by bartering land or ornaments.

Many trade sisters and even daughters for other wives for themselves.

Old wives do not welcome a younger one in the family; the young bride is often tortured by the first wife. If the husband learns of this the first wife loses her authority in the household. Polygamy is not generally practiced, however, because women are in the minority. In the north and central parts of Australia, courteous husbands lend their wives to a guest. They prefer, however, to lend them to a white man, being jealous of one of their own people.

Fat women are most popular and are often abducted by the natives. Even though ugly, obese women are always preferred. Slender thighs are regarded with disgust by the fat-loving aborigines. This love for adipose tissue is a characteristic of most savages, especially among the Africans, Orientals and many of the tribes of the South Sea Islands. Men admire plumpness and excessive fat in women for sensual purposes.

MARRIAGE CUSTOMS OF THE MAORIS OF NEW ZEALAND

The Maoris of to-day are nearly all Christians, but their religion formerly consisted of nature and ancestral worship. They then believed in a hereafter, and thought that the soul dwelt in the left eye. They did not believe in any gods, and they had no temples of worship.

The Maoris practiced cannibalism and ate the hearts of their victims to gain their courage and strength. They, like the Fijians, reveled in the taste of human flesh, often the chief part of their diet. Members of the family, however, were never in any danger of being killed.

When a man desired a certain woman to be his wife, he had to capture her. His friends assisted him in pursuing her until she was actually in their hands. If a girl had previously run away with a man she liked, because her parents had refused their consent, she was often brought back by the suitor who was favored by the parents and a "pulling-fight" took place, the girl being placed between the two men, each trying to pull her from the other, often injuring the girl fatally. In many cases, the weakening suitor, losing his bride, would throw his spear into her heart to end her suffering and to revenge himself on his rival.

Child betrothals are uncommon to-day. The Maoris of New Zealand were polygamous but are now monogamous in the strictest sense. They have great respect for their wives and consult them on every matter of importance. Girls marry very young, and the bridegroom is not often older than seventeen.

The Maoris do not like to intermarry with other tribes; therefore, consanguineous marriages are frequent. Foreigners may marry Maori women but a white woman has never been known to marry a Maori.

Their savage instincts have quite vanished; they are now a kind and obedient people though lazy. Formerly, infanticide was practiced, and mothers preferred to suckle pigs and puppies, rather than to raise children. In times of war, women often joined in the battles.

When there are children, a man very seldom divorces his wife. When a man died, his wife or wives would go to his oldest brother. Female children had no rights to their father's property.

MARRIAGE CUSTOMS OF FIJI

Before the Europeans definitely settled in Fiji, ancestor-worship and the belief in a future state after death, combined with cannibalism, lead the natives to commit unspeakable atrocities. They loved the taste of human flesh, and the chiefs did not stop at slaughtering relatives and friends in order to gratify their insatiable appetites. These customs have greatly changed, and cannibalism is not indulged in freely at the present time. The women, who were looked upon as slaves, were forbidden to join the ceremonies of worship and were not allowed to enter any places of worship. The Fijians killed the old and the crippled.

Fijians believe that if they are not tattooed, their god Dengei will seek vengeance upon them after death. They are also firmly convinced that the god Nangganangga, who watches over married people, will not let any bachelor enter the Fijian paradise and will reduce them to ashes if they are not married when they die. Practically everyone is therefore married in Fiji. Men were not permitted to marry young at one time, although they were often betrothed before birth.

Girls, on the other hand, were married when very young because they were betrothed to older men. The parents often gave their daughters in marriage to men who were sometimes three and four times older than the girls. This condition still prevails to-day. Parents and husbands do not hesitate to barter their daughters or wives to redeem themselves of debts or any other obligations. Fathers repeat this old proverb to their sons-in-law, "If you become discontented with her, sell her; kill her; eat her; you are the absolute master."

The peculiar shape of the heads of many of the natives of Fiji is due to the fact that mothers still deform their babies' skulls at birth to make them more "beautiful."

When old enough, girls must have dots burned on their arms and backs as a decoration, alluring to men. Girls wear only a girdle, five to six inches wide, made of hibiscus bark and dyed in varied colors. As soon as they have had their first child, they lengthen their girdles into moderately long skirts.

In olden days, a chief had from twenty to a hundred wives, and at his death, wives and slaves were buried with him to accompany him to the next world.

The women who have intermarried with Europeans are usually prolific, and the children born are nearly all scrofulous. One per cent of the natives are estimated to be lepers. Male children are always preferred; and when a boy is old enough, he is taught by his father to beat his mother as a sign of superiority.

MARRIAGE CUSTOMS OF SAMOA

Though most Samoans have become Christians, in their religious ceremonies remain the superstitious ideas which were formerly associated with their primitive religion. They believe that after death their spirits travel through a subterranean passage on the west side of Savaii, one of the largest islands of the fourteen of the Samoan group, where all spirits meet and rejoice. The cannibalism practiced among the primitive Samoans was not as rapacious as that of the Fijians, for cannibalism was only practiced in that portion of their religious ceremonies demanding human beings for sacrifice. A woman or a child was never killed.

The Samoans and Tongas are recognized as the finest type of Polynesians; the women are pretty and the men are supposed to be the tallest in the world. They are highly intelligent, generous, and hospitable. They make excellent warriors, sailors, and boat builders.

At birth, children's frontal bones are flattened, and their bones pressed out of shape to form flat heads and noses, a requirement of beauty.

The Samoan men observe the custom of tattooing their bodies from the navel to the thighs, and sometimes around the mouth and eyes. Formerly, a man who was not tattooed was not eligible as a husband, for tattooing was the distinctive sign of manhood.

A chief was once allowed to use the daughters of his wife's relatives who lived in his household, as concubines. A woman, chosen against her will, usually left the chief's roof as soon after the wedding ceremony as possible, to choose a husband.

Chastity was strictly enforced. When a

woman was not a virgin at marriage, she was beaten and abused in many other ways at a public ceremony of verification. She was then sent back to her parents who were also considered disgraced. On the other hand, if she had retained her virtue, she was rewarded with many gifts. No apparent mode of courtship other than mutual sniffing is known.

The custom of proving a woman's chastity prevailed only among the chiefs. Among the lower classes, the loss of a woman's virtue was not looked upon with such severity. There were no inhibitions, and examples of obscenities were frequent, especially in the family itself. Girls were at liberty to cohabit with foreigners, although they were not allowed to do so with the natives. Abortions were often resorted to.

Circumcision of boys at the age of puberty is common to many tribes. A peculiar operation, similar to the circumcision of the male, is made upon girls at the same period to remove any excess flesh and to frustrate erotic desires during adolescence.

To-day, among some of the Samoan clans, the strictest decorum is observed in the home. Children are not allowed to utter a word which might have an indecent meaning.

When a man has several wives, each woman, in turn, lives with him for three days, a custom also observed by the Zulu-Kaffirs of Africa. No distinction as to closeness of relationship is made between brothers, sisters or cousins, while an aunt and an uncle are called, respectively: "mother" and "father."

If a divorced woman wishes to remarry, she must have the approval of her first husband. Infanticide prevailed on some of the smaller islands to prevent over population, although this custom does not exist to-day.

An adulterer was often killed by the offended husband or by a member of the tribe.

MARRIAGE CUSTOMS OF TAHITI

Tahitians belong to the Polynesian race and resemble the Marquesans; but most of their customs and beliefs are decidedly different from those of the latter.

Circumcision and tattooing are generally practiced among some of the natives of to-day; these customs have not yet vanished. The tattooed designs which are ornamental always interpret some superstitious custom or belief, and emphasize the contours of the natural lines of the body. These designs are usually tattooed on girls and boys at the beginning of the adolescent period. The more elaborate the patterns, the more dignified is the person considered. Anyone without the customary tattooing is looked upon with disgust.

Frederick O'Brien, in "Mystic Isles of the South Seas" writes that the method of wearing a flower may convey various messages. If a girl wants a lover, she wears a flower over her left ear; a blossom placed on the right, indicates happiness.

Before Europeans came to Tahiti, infanticide was practiced by all the natives, and, although not of a cannibalistic nature, human sacrifices were part of their worship. Flat, wide noses were considered beautiful, and mothers resorted to many practices to conform the noses of their children to this standard. The older girls fared badly on this island of the South Seas, for if they were unable to assist the men in their daily tasks and could not fight in the wars, they were put to death. This accounts for the predominance of the male sex. If a woman of rank married to an inferior had a child, it was immediately killed. If an unmarried man became the father of a child, he was considered married if he did not kill the infant instantly.

Throughout the Islands of the Pacific, the beauty of Tahitian women is unequaled. But, because of their sensuous living, the bloom of youth fades quickly. Another cause is the bearing of many children beginning almost from the first days of puberty.

Although brides are not bought in Tahiti, the gifts from a suitor to the girl's father represent more or less the price of a wife.

As soon as a girl is betrothed, she is secluded on a high platform built in the house for this purpose. She is kept away from every one; her food is brought to her, and she remains there with nothing to do. On very rare occasions, she is permitted to leave the house, but only with the greatest care and discretion, and accompanied by one of her relatives. The wedding is the occasion for the display of all the family relics, such as weapons, bones, sharks' teeth, etc. White cloths are the customary gifts to the bride.

At the wedding ceremony, in response to the usual questions as to their willingness to marry, both bride and bridegroom answer "No" instead of "Yes".

Though at the present time, divorce is simple, a married man who has a child will not divorce or leave his wife. In old Tahiti, the custom of concubinage was practiced among the higher classes as it was in most tribes of the South Seas.

MARRIAGE CUSTOMS OF HAWAII

Hawaiians never thought of marriage as a lasting union.

The women were lascivious and hated to bear children because that interfered with their dancing and feasting, often resorting to abortions and infanticide. Many instances are known of women suckling pigs and dogs. Men were not cruel to the women; but all females were excluded, at the risk of being killed, from sharing food with them or from entering the temples. The women, often self-willed, seem incapable of great love for their husbands.

The exchange of wives among friends was a sign of friendship; fat women being greatly desired, having a reputation for sexual abandon. Almost all married women had public lovers called "punula"; and the nightly gatherings for the hula hula dance were marked by passionate moments, definitely obscene to the Western point of view.

MARRIAGE CUSTOMS OF THE PAPUANS OF NEW GUINEA

The Papuans of British New Guinea live like birds in tiny huts perched in tall trees and called "dobbos", each family having its separate dwelling. In the north of the Island (German New Guinea) the huts are usually built on piles, but the roofs of bamboo or palm are so low that they almost touch the ground. In the west, (Dutch New Guinea) large houses five hundred to seven hundred feet long are built wherein dwell many families. Others are built two stories high, but the most common house is built on piles, and measures from sixty to seventy feet long.

Very few of the Papuans have been converted to a formal religion; most of the natives are still pagans.

Papuan parents, too, often promise their daughters in marriage before they are born, but, in most cases, girls are purchased by their suitors at the marriageable age.

A great feast is given to initiate boys and girls who have reached the age of puberty. For this occasion, masks are worn. In all their festivities, although pleasure loving and fond of music, the Papuans rarely sing.

Girls believe that, in order to command the admiration of men, they must be tattooed. As an additional lure they also file their teeth to a sharp point.

Friends of the suitor formerly used to assist in the pretended capture of the bride. Even now these elopements occur. When the couple returns, they are forgiven after the bridegroom pays the customary price to his bride's parents.

Among some of the Papuan tribes, men may only marry in their own villages; other groups permit marriages only to women of the tribe from which the suitor's mother came.

Among some clans of the smaller islands of the Malayan Archipelago, a girl was expected to give up her luxuriant hair at betrothal and to refrain from wearing any garments. This custom has almost disappeared. Before the girl is married, she has certain parts of her body tattooed; her face must be tattooed after the marriage to mark her as a married woman. The men may not be tattooed until they have killed another man. Sometimes scars are raised on the arms and breast to mark unusual experiences at sea.

For the newly married couple to live together immediately after the ceremony would be considered immodest. This custom has also been observed by the Brazilian aborigines.

A new wife may be acquired only with the consent of the other wives. Divorce is rare, although both husband and wife are free to dissolve the marriage when they please. The women of some tribes leave their husbands intermittently to live with other men.

Papuans hate large families and abortion is practiced. "Children are a burden," is a proverbial expression, "they destroy us." This hatred is undoubtedly due to the fact that the women do most of the work and child-bearing is, therefore, too great a burden. In Papua, girls are saved from death, in preference to boys, because the bride-price eventually brings wealth to the parents.

The natives are very superstitious, wear amulets to protect themselves from the evil spirits, believe in sorcerers and charms, and practice ancestral worship. They are generally uneducated; only a few can count to five and most of them not at all.

The men arrange their frizzled, woolly hair either on the top of the head mop-style or separate it in small bunches, each tied with vegetable fiber strings from the base through to the full length of the hair. Sometimes many hundreds of these upright bunches decorate a man's head. Although the bodies are covered with hair, the faces are hairless.

Few clothes are worn and except for the loincloth made out of the hibiscus or other plants or a girdle, the people are nude. Among some tribes, men and women wear a cushion, on which they can sit, hanging in the back from the waist. In the northeast and west of New Guinea, women wear a skirt open on the hip to display their tattooing.

Men love to display ornaments at festivals. These are made by themselves, and include earrings of shells, a coronet of dogs' teeth, and a huge characteristic Papuan comb, made of bamboo decorated with brilliant feathers. They glory in tying in their long hair, as many of the bones of their victims as they can carry. To complete this bizzare, ceremonial costume, a bone, a feather, or a piece of shell is worn through the septum of the nose.

MARRIAGE CUSTOMS IN THE MALAY ARCHIPELAGO

Paganism reigned supreme among the Malays until the beginning of the thirteenth century, when Mohammedanism was introduced. Many have been converted, yet most of the customs and beliefs include pagan rites. Among several of the Malay tribes, many of the ceremonies resemble those of the Hindus, whose customs were introduced in the Malay Archipelago by the traders.

Early marriages are common to the peoples of all Islands of the Malay Archipelago. When a girl reaches the age of puberty, her teeth are filed as a sign of her eligibility to become a wife. Before marrying, she blackens them to enhance her personal charm. Kissing is unknown among the natives.

A custom of Sumatra, called "ambol ank," allowed the father of a virgin the right to select her mate and to retain him in his house as a son and debtor. This mode of marriage sometimes endured, but generally the union lasted for only a few years. The husband was then permitted to take his wife to his own home. Sometimes the wife refused to go with him due to the influence of her parents who preferred to have her remain with them. If she stayed, she could be sold again to another suitor. The first husband had no right to any of the presents or property earned during the period of servitude. The children resulting from the union remained with the wife.

Another mode of marriage called "somando" sanctioned the union on terms of equality, permitting the couple to live as they pleased.

Among other tribes, a third form of marriage called "jujur" which is still practiced today, consists of acquiring a bride by purchase or barter.

Marriage by capture is the most commonly practiced form of marriage of the present day. Elsewhere in the islands, before a suitor is accepted he must go through the ceremony of answering questions as to his prowess to hunt, fish and climb trees, and as to his worldly possessions which are then given to the bride's parents. For this occasion the bridegroom is dressed in bark, fiber, and the indispensable necklace of an animal's teeth.

Another marriage called "tolari gadis," not

sanctioned by the law, is that following an elopement, disregarding the wishes of the parents.

When a man discovers that his wife is not a virgin, he sends her back to her parents. When she becomes old, he replaces her with a younger wife.

Among some tribes, when the husband dies, his property reverts to his brothers and sisters rather than to his own children. Among a few of the Sumatra tribes, when a man wants more than one wife, he barters his sisters and marriageable daughters for a new bride.

Among most of the tribes, a man may repudiate his wife only upon the grounds of adultery, but a woman may divorce her husband on the grounds of ill-treatment or unfaithfulness. Adultery is not considered a serious crime and is usually only subject to a fine.

The lower classes are monogamous; only among the higher class does polygamy and concubinage exist. Among some tribes, unions of brothers and sisters are sanctioned.

Whenever a Menangkabos husband has the number of wives allowed by the Koran, he lives at the home of his parents and makes but a weekly visit to each of his wives.

When a Menangkabos girl marries she remains with her mother. For her purposes, a small hut is put up contiguous to the mother's home. As each daughter weds, an addition is built in which she lives and raises her children. This explains the picturesque cluster of pronged roofs which is characteristic of the Menangkabos settlements. The husband assists in cultivating the plot of land which is the mother's gift to the bride.

MARRIAGE CUSTOMS OF JAVA

The Javanese have many marriage customs similar to those of the Malays of Sumatra, including the filing and blackening of the girl's teeth as an aid to charm. Their marriage feasts, however, are of a more artistic nature for they are natural musicians. Their orchestras, called "gamelin," have wind, string, and percussion instruments.

Native princes and sovereigns have but one wife, though they may have several concubines. The Chinese often marry Javanese and half-caste girls. Although a Dutch woman may not marry a Javanese, Dutch men do, and the children are respected though they do not enjoy social prestige. Celibacy is almost unknown. Boys and girls marry when eleven or twelve years of age, and the majority of them raise large families; but due to the lack of hygienic conditions, infant mortality is high.

Courtship takes place at the end of the harvest season when the work in the field has been completed. After the parents of the bride have received the customary gifts of food, clothes, and cooking utensils, the bridegroom has to stand up to his chin in water while he recites traditional lines to the priest of the mosque. On the three days previous to the wedding, the bride may eat only "three teaspoonsful of rice and drink but a cup of hot water a day."

For the wedding ceremony, the Javanese bride has her hair oiled and plaited into long, thick braids, entwined with jasmine flowers. A white, native rice-powder is used by the Javanese bride as a symbol of purity. Her face is completely covered with it, while her shoulders and arms are covered with a yellow salve called "boreh."

The bridegroom's preparations consist of filing his teeth and blackening them with lacquer. He is also smeared with "boreh," and jasmine wreaths and silver ornaments complete his bridal costume. He is then ready to call for his bride who is awaiting him at her parents' home. When they finally meet, the bride kneels and washes the bridegroom's feet in sign of servitude. She then sits on a mat which has been placed in the middle of the road for this occasion. Sometimes two fowls are sacrificed, and the blood is sprinkled upon the head and shoulders of the married couple.

When a woman decides to have a certain man as her lover and is successful in luring him to eat with her, she places in his food a love philter which she has previously concocted. The Javanese women are of a very jealous nature, and if a lover tires of her before her admiration for him has ceased, she will seek vengeance until her wrath is finally appeased by desire for another man.

MARRIAGE CUSTOMS OF THE DYAKS OF BORNEO

In the Dyak's village near the sea, houses are built in the water, and on market days canoes are used as stalls. Floating villages are not unusual, and the natives enter and leave their unsteady habitations with ease and confidence.

The savage tribes in the interior of Borneo recognize one god named "Sang-Sang," and a large number of subordinate deities, but there are neither places of worship nor priests; all rites are performed by the father of each family.

At one time, about a year before the age of puberty, Dutch Borneo girls were imprisoned for several years in a dark room. No one was permitted to see them except the mother and the

female slave who brought them food and sup-
plied them with materials for the mats they made
during their captivity. When these girls were
brought into the daylight after many years of seclusion, their skin had become a sickly, saffron
shade, and they were very thin and feeble. This
was supposed, however, to enhance their charms
in the eyes of the native men and they soon
found husbands.

At present, girls of Borneo enjoy greater liberty, but they must work hard during their
youth and suffer great physical pain under the
strain of their daily tasks. They marry at about
thirteen years of age, bear many children, do
most of the work, and are poorly fed. These
girls who have beauty and strength when they
marry are soon transformed into old, deformed,
and sickly-looking women.

If signs of pregnancy appear, an unmarried
girl can quickly find a husband, because it is
evident that she is not barren; and the men of
Borneo prefer to marry when they are certain
to have offspring. In that case, the bridegroom
sends as many gifts to her parents as he can
afford; and the marriage is immediately arranged.

Girls have many love affairs before marriage
and appear to have a free hand in selecting their
husbands. Upon marriage, they are usually faith-

ful. Dyaks may have but one wife, and unfaithfulness is punished by a slight fine.

A Dyak, when courting a girl, usually calls at her home during the night. He wakes her and when they become acquainted, he shares her bed. If they are pleased with one another and can obtain the consent of her parents, who are usually aware of the sexual experiments, the couple is then married.

"Be good enough to blow up the fire," is an expression of refusal to a nocturnal suitor's advances.

In some parts of Borneo, notably Upper Sarawak, most men and women are polygamous. Adultery is commonly practiced, and any reason is sufficient to secure a divorce.

An unmarried man must live alone in a large hut in the center of the village. As a pre-requisite to marriage, a man must have at least one skull decorating his hut. Prior to going head-hunting, he must participate in a ceremony in a tabooed hut. On his expedition, he wears the skins of wild animals and a mask.

A husband who desires a son must present his wife with the skull of one of his own tribesmen.

The Moros of Mindanao in the Philippine Islands use a special knife called "canpilan" on brutal hunts, a knife sharp enough to slice off a head with one stroke. The favorite heirloom is a skull with a perfect jaw. The man with the largest collection of skulls is accorded the greatest authority and respect.

MARRIAGE CUSTOMS IN THE PHILIPPINE ISLANDS

The boys and girls of the primitive tribes in the interior of Luzon, Panay, Mindanao, and Negros of the Philippine Islands must undergo the ceremony of tattooing at the age of puberty.

The Igorots who were the aborigines of the Malay Archipelago are the present inhabitants of Luzon and vicinity. Head-hunting is still practiced here. Most of the inhabitants are capable agriculturists.

Although the Igorots of Luzon consider the chastity of a woman as indispensable, the betrothal is never taken seriously until the bride is pregnant.

The Igorots are monogamous; if a man is found guilty of adultery, he is forced into exile, never to return either to his tribe or to his family.

Marriage between close relatives is generally forbidden; and those with dark complexions never marry those of a lighter color.

If, after the purchase of their wives, the Bagobos of the Philippine Islands are satisfied with them, the bride's father refunds one half

of the purchase money or gifts. Stranger still, is
the first wife's rejoicing on the arrival of a second one; another person in the household light-
ens the burden of her domestic duties.

CHAPTER IV

MYSTERY PEOPLES

MARRIAGE CUSTOMS OF THE GYPSIES

SOME authorities maintain that the
Gypsies originated in Lower Egypt,
while a few believe that they came
from India. Grellman, one of the best informed
authorities, is of the opinion that they came
from Hindostan. When Timus Beg introduced
the Mohammedan religion (about A.D. 1408-
1400), thousands were killed, imprisoned, or
made slaves; the others escaped such punishments
by migrating to other lands.

Gypsies usually adopt the religious customs
and beliefs of the country in which they live.
Yet they are always half pagan and superstitious
by nature. They do not believe in the Ten Com-
mandments: they call God, "Devla," the devil,
"Bang," and the Cross, "Trushul."

In Transylvania, to marry, the bride breaks
a dish at the feet of the bridegroom before a

judge or gako. The pieces are gathered and pre-
served. These must not be lost or destroyed, because the union would then no longer be binding; they would be forced to remarry, perform-
ing the same ceremony.

Among the Spanish gypsies, the suitor,
usually selected by the girl's parents, is not allowed to court his fiancée. If they happen to see
each other, they meet merely as acquaintances.
Formerly, if a betrothed girl wandered from the
path of virtue, the irate father often killed her.
At present, the father metes out a severe punishment.

George Borrow, in his "Gypsies in Spain,"
describes one of their wedding festivities: "To
the gypsy, a wedding is an important affair, because only a married man counts in the tribe. If
he be rich, he often becomes poor before it is
terminated, frequently involving himself for
life, in order to procure the means of giving a
festival; without a festival he could not be a
Rom, that is, a husband, and would cease to belong to the sect of Romany.

"Drinking, dancing, feasting, and singing go
on all day, but the gist of the festival is at night.
Nearly a ton-weight of sweetmeats is prepared,
of all kinds and forms, principally yolks of eggs
with a crust of sugar, and these are strewn on
the floor of a large room to the depth of three

inches. In a few minutes after the dancing has begun the sweetmeats are reduced to powder, or rather mud, and the dancers are soiled to the knees with sugar, fruit, and yolks of eggs. This festival lasts three days, at the end of which the bridegroom has dissipated most of his property."

In Hungary, gypsy weddings greatly resemble those of Transylvania. A chief is presented with a jug of red wine; after he has tasted it he touches the lips of the couple with wine; the chief then hurls the jug as far as he can. It breaks into pieces, and the "wise women" who are present at weddings, hasten to count them. The more fragments there are, the more chances there are for a long life for the wedded couple.

The only marriage ceremony among the Gypsies of England, is for the father of the bride to hold a broom over which the couple must jump; thus they become man and wife.

Intermarriage in the family is usually avoided, yet it has been known for a brother to marry his sister. Gypsy girls have love affairs but they would be dishonored if they had a child out of wedlock.

MARRIAGE CUSTOMS OF THE NORTH AMERICAN INDIANS

The Indians' knowledge of nature has never yet been surpassed by the white men. Each

deed was a studied effort to combat the exacti-
tudes of primitive nature. Their daily routine
was a struggle to provide sustenance, clothe
themselves, and to dispel the evil spirits with
their barbaric incantations. Their courtship was
not of a romantic nature, and they married
exclusively for procreation. Strong women were,
therefore, greatly desired.

MARRIAGE CUSTOMS OF THE NAVAJO AND APACHE INDIANS

The Navajo Indians, who number approximately twenty-five thousand, believe that "their
bones would dry up and they would die" if they
intermarried. They practiced polygamy unre-
servedly, having as many as five wives. Girls
are betrothed at an early age and marry when
very young. The bride price is paid in horses.
Twelve is considered the highest price and is
paid only if the bride is beautiful and has proved
of excellent domestic qualities. Eating pudding
from the same dish constituted the marriage
ceremony. A married woman is free to leave her
husband if she has good reasons.

Married women own the greater part of the
property. The husband's belongings consist only
of weapons, many ornaments, a saddle and horse,
and the proverbial blanket which never leaves

him. The wife has exclusive rights to all live-stock. A cultivated cornfield is presented to her by her family or clan, or the husband must prepare land which will afterward belong to his wife for cultivation.

The husband has no authority over his children, and if either he or his wife dies, the property goes to the nephews and nieces. When a brother wishes to present his sister with a gift, it must first be placed on the ground and may not be passed directly. This is the only taboo observed.

Among the Apache Indians the women are generally chaste. Chiefs may have as many wives as they can afford, one always remaining the favorite. His importance is measured by the number of his wives.

The levirate custom of marrying the brother's widow is observed, but the wedding must occur within a year of the death. If it does not, the widow may marry the man of her choice.

The Navajo and Apache Indians will never eat fish, bears, wild turkeys or the flesh of swine.

MARRIAGE CUSTOMS OF THE CHEROKEE INDIANS

The Cherokee Indians of Oklahoma are nearly all of mixed blood. Those of the reservation of

North Carolina are called the Eastern Band. This tribe is to-day recognized as having been one of the most civilized of all.

George Gist or Guess (Sequoya), a mixed blood Cherokee Indian, invented a syllabic alphabet in 1821 which enabled his people to learn to read and write.

The few remaining old Cherokee Indians cling to their old superstitions, ancient rites, and sacred traditions.

MARRIAGE CUSTOMS OF THE INDIANS OF VANCOUVER ISLANDS

The suitor, accompanied by his friends, paddled at the head of a procession of forty canoes to the home of the bride of his choice. Arriving at the beach of her tribe, the men remained silent until they were asked the reason for their call.

One of the suitor's friends then rose from his seat in the canoe and, as loudly as he could, he told the reason for the call, extolling the qualifications of his friend.

The canoes were paddled ashore, and several blankets were given to the parents of the girl as first payment. The girl's tribe, however, derided the gift and a brave stepped forward from the shore to tell, in sonorous tones, of the girl's charms, virtue and beauty.

After another gift had been made, the girl was stripped of her clothing, and, clad only in her under-garments, was given to her future husband who covered her with a blanket. This was the only ceremonial of marriage, though the rite was not considered consummated until she bore a child.

Adultery or concubinage was punishable by death, the punishment being inflicted by the father or the brother of the guilty person. Husbands often loaned their wives to guests, however, and women were often exchanged for property.

MARRIAGE CUSTOMS OF THE ESKIMOS OF GREENLAND

Though the Eskimos married children of five years of age, the marriage was not recognized until a child had been born. At the age of puberty, boys and girls were tattooed and painted, and the septum of the nose was pierced to insert the labrets, usually pieces of shell or wood.

The Eskimos of Eastern Greenland still practice marriage by capture. There is no courtship among them; even the rubbing of noses is no longer practiced. Mothers sometimes still show affection for their children by such a demonstration.

The girl must always answer "No" to a proposal, for an immediate affirmative answer would be immodest. There is no marriage ceremony or other formality of any kind.

Polygamy is rarely practiced among them, but the sterility of a wife will often cause a man to add another wife to his household. In no instance, however, will a man forsake a pregnant wife. Here, too, a woman is offered to a guest as a sign of hospitality. The Eskimos of Newfoundland are not demonstrative towards their wives, but they do not ill-treat them.

In Greenland, on the contrary, a husband does not hesitate to beat his wife when she displeases him, but he would resent her correcting his children's errors.

MARRIAGE CUSTOMS OF THE SIOUX INDIANS

When a man chooses the daughter of a Sioux chief, he marries the whole family, for he has the right to possess any daughters or sisters of his wife as soon as they are of a marriageable age. When he has chosen a girl, he sends her a gift which is the equivalent of a promise of marriage, and a month later they go on a hunting trip which is their honeymoon. On their return, any game that has been killed is offered to the parents for their approval.

The Sioux Indians were one of the least savage tribes of the Northern tribes. Their song lore was of a romantic and peaceful nature. Marriages were often dissolved if no children were born. Among some of the American Indians, incestuous marriages sometimes took place.

Among many of the northern Indians, a woman could propose to the man she preferred. To accomplish her ends, she built a fire and baked a cake near his tent. When it was done, if he shared it with her, it constituted the marriage ceremony, and he then invited her into his tent.

Youths were married at about twelve years of age, and celibacy was practically unknown. The isolation of newly born babies and their mothers was a taboo strictly adhered to by many tribes.

The Indians of Oregon and Washington advertised for a wife by carving human figures on trees. Another mode of proposal by the suitor was to throw the game killed in the hunt at the door of the girl. Thus he proved to her that he was a capable hunter, and perfectly able to provide for a family.

THE END